IN THE SHADOW OF HI

IN THE SHADOW OF HIS WINGS

The Pastoral Ministry of Angels:
Yesterday, Today, and for Heaven

JONATHAN MACY

Lewis

May the Lord bless you in your
ministry — and may you be an
angel of the Lord to those
in need.

CASCADE *Books* · Eugene, Oregon

IN THE SHADOW OF HIS WINGS
The Pastoral Ministry of Angels: Yesterday, Today, and for Heaven

Cascade Books
An Imprint of Wipf and Stock Publishers
199 W. 8th Ave., Suite 3
Eugene, OR 97401

www. wipfandstock.com

ISBN 13: 978-1-60899-837-1

Cataloging-in-Publication data:

Macy, Jonathan.
    In the shadow of his wings : the pastoral ministry of angels: yesterday, today, and for heaven / Jonathan Macy.
    xii + 160 p. ; cm. 23 — Includes bibliographical references and index.
    ISBN 13: 978-1-60899-837-1
    1. Angels. 2. Angels—Biblical teaching. I. Title.

BL477 M27 2011

Manufactured in the U.S.A.

For Louiz

I remember the exhibition where your prayers sat, beautifully lit, beneath the shadow of God's wings; prayers which you had made by hand, and individually prayed. As you prayed, Jesus watched you and smiled. And as he saw your incense rise, the angels too saw this scene and rejoiced, since you were joining with them in one of the great works of heaven. Thank you for walking with me on my journey of Life.

CONTENTS

Tʜɪs ʙᴏᴏᴋ ᴡᴀs ᴀ long time coming. If I thought there was anything in astrology, then I would say that many planets had to come into conjunction for it to happen. But I don't. I do, however, believe in a God of grace and good gifts, who has taken me on a journey over many years, and who has weaved many wonderful strands of my life together to get me to this point. Some of those strands are described in this book, others are not. Yet God knows the tapestry called "Jonathan" he has designed, and so I thank him, first and foremost, for everything I am and for my life. I hope and pray that this book does some justice to that unseen part of his Creation we so often simply miss or ignore, and opens eyes previously closed to the mystery and majesty the God's angels.

As with any book, but especially the first, there are many people to thank and acknowledge. First, those who read through my drafts, making many helpful comments. I begin with my Mum, Caroline. I have been ever so fortunate to have a professional proof reader for a Mum! She has always willingly read and questioned my many dissertations over the years, including at short notice, and her fresh and skilled eyes have always picked out errors, clumsinesses(!) and inconsistencies. She has been an important part of my development, especially in teaching me how to write English proper! And thanks too to both Mum and Dad (Nicholas) for raising me to have an inquiring mind, interested in all things seen and unseen.

Next is Steve Morris, for not only encouraging me to find my writing voice and offering important insights, but also for numerous encouraging words over my two years at Wycliffe. We met on the first week and forged a good and deep friendship which has lasted.

Thank you to Liz Hoare for being such a great scholar and tutor, whose reflective, spiritual faith always encouraged me at Wycliffe. It was her insight that my time at Wycliffe was a gift from God to wisely use that finally spurred me into action and writing. Liz helped me on numerous projects and also spent a wonderful term walking with me through the Parables. That she also read my drafts with joy and vision was a fantastic bonus. Also, thank you to her husband Toddy. His views from another perspective were also helpful.

Simon Ponsonby, who not only fed me with his preaching while at St Aldates, but who also read this book carefully and prayer-fully. To have a man of his calibre read my work was a real honour, and his encouragement a deep blessing. Our friendship will continue.

Martyn Casserly, my interested and able non-expert, who was my guinea-pig. His insights into flow and balance were really helpful.

Justin Hardin, who read through my work on Hebrews 1:14. He, along with other Wycliffe tutors (especially Peter Walker, who was always on hand with wise words), were a great encouragement to me as I engaged on this flight of fancy! These readers were invaluable to the final shape of the book.

A nod must also go to Dan Naulty for being a friend and sounding board for my whackier ideas. He soon learnt that everything (yes, everything!), eventually, comes back to angels. The dungeon at Wycliffe (not forgetting Kosta and Christian) was always a great place for saintly wisdom, strange humour, and strong coffee.

My college roommate Tom Rout deserves many thanks, for patiently putting up with me for two years breaking the studious silence with "*Could I ask you something?* . . ." and then rambling off on countless tangents and dead-end paths about theophanies, Christophanies, and pillars of cloud. More than he knows, he helped hone many things in this book.

I must also recognise my spiritual formation—we all come from somewhere. Not only this book, but myself as person, is the product of a long journey. So thank you to Steve Woodger who led me to Christ all those years ago; Epping Forest Community Church for the early discipleship and fellowship; City Hope (especially Dave and Lesley, and Martyn, but many others besides, too numerous to list), and Christ Church Camberwell (Hugh and Helen Balfour, Adrian Jervis, ManGroup, and everybody else there who like the stars that are beyond counting!) which became more than just a spiritual home, but also a launch-pad into God's calling on my life. And finally, Phil Rogers and St. John's Plumstead. Thank you for welcoming us all also warmly.

Thanks must also go to Rudi Heinze and Martin Davie for being so inspiring at Oak Hill; Richard Price and Anthony Meredith (Heythrop College) for a thorough postgraduate grounding to prepare me for doctoral work; Graham Gould for working with me through my PhD at King's College London; and of course the staff at Wycliffe Hall who gave me confidence on this journey.

Thank you also to Michael Perham, Bishop of Gloucester, who found time to chat with me about his "angelic" work in Common Worship, and to write an endorsement for this book. Similarly, deep and heartfelt thanks must go to Rachel Hickson (Heart Cry Ministries), Justyn Terry (Dean and President: Trinity School for Ministry, Pennsylvania) and Simon Ponsonby (Pastor Of Theology: St. Aldates, Oxford) for kindly agreeing to read and endorse the book. None of them had to do so, and for them to offer their time and expertise to a cold-calling "nobody" like me has been both amazing and humbling. Their gracious support, kind words and encouragements have blessed me very much. Thank you.

Thank you to my prayer team who, over the last few years, have been there whenever I have called upon them. Those not already mentioned: Julie and David McGregor; Young and Paul Lee; Dan Poulson; Dez Gray; Chris Sewell; Stef Liston; Julian Kelly; Matthias Benz; Andy Exelby; Louise and Dave Crocombe; Paul and Becs Whittlesea; Gillian and Peter Corfield; Phil and Marie Anne Joiner; the Christchurch crew, including Steph, and Chris and Claire. Your prayers, added to those of the angels, have made all the difference.

Last, but not least, Louiz, Joel and Emma. Words, in this case, are not enough.

INTRODUCTION: ALL THINGS SEEN AND UNSEEN

LUNCHTIMES AT COLLEGE WERE always great times for throwing around ideas and discussing whatever you might be working on at the time. No matter what one might be doing, you could always count on somebody to make a worthwhile comment.

During one such lunchtime I was chatting with one of my fellow students about angels, and he told me something Francis Schaeffer had once written: "In the first few minutes of any conversation, mention angels." Mention angels!?! Why? The reason was simple. All too often people think that Christianity is simply a moral or ethical code or philosophy, and our conversations are usually framed that way as well. However, it is so much more than this, and the introduction of angels into any conversation immediately flags up loud and clear that we are not dealing with a set of rules to follow, but with something fundamentally other-worldly.

Christianity is not just a system of thought to ensure people are nice to each other, but naturally has something of the transcendent. Angels force one to consider the supernatural and mystical. Angels tear the heavens open and begin to reveal the heart of the creation and the riches of God toward it—a created order that is truly magnificent and truly spiritual. There is more to this life than we can see. In fact, angels state this so comprehensively that in a modern and rational world where you only believe in that which you can touch, hold, and analyse, they have become a subject of discomfort and ridicule. This is a tension I personally feel.

Many years ago I wrote my PhD about angels, and I am often asked what I learned from doing that. This question usually elicits two conflicting responses. The first is to face the fact that my PhD is sitting in its nice blue cover on a shelf in my living room gathering dust. Over numerous years, it has never helped me in any sermon, in any prayer, nor in any pastoral conversation, situation, or activity. Not once. It seemingly has no use in the service of the church or for other Christians: a fascinating folly; a classic white elephant.

Yet, the second reaction is that it tore wide-open my whole view of creation—that the Creed's statement of a belief in the created unseen actually meant something tangible and real, and this tangible reality touches on our day-to-day lives. Angels are not an abstract or fanciful theory, but heavenly ministers of God's blessings. Creation used to be a 2D monochrome picture. True, black and white pictures can be stunningly beautiful, highly detailed, and able to conjure deep emotions within, and I had lived with this for years. Now, however, creation is truly 3D and in Technicolor; a huge tapestry of enormous depth and richness. I realised there was more than I could ever comprehend going on around me. More than this, it caught the imagination of non-Christians more than that of Christians. Theology, religion, and church bored them rigid—all so irrelevant. But, angels? Huh? "*Tell me more!*"

Such is the often topsy-turvy world of angels and angelology. Ridicule and fascination in equal proportion, and these usually spring from unexpected quarters. We live in a world where people are less interested in whether something is true, and more in whether it works—"*How will this change my life?*" Theory is less important than application, and with angels this is particularly pertinent. For many centuries, in fact for the vast majority of church history, discussions of angels have been framed in the abstract and theological, the mystical and mysterious, and not in the pastoral and practical. It is a methodology (essentially rooted in early church speculation, and refined by medieval scholasticism) that has revelled in theological investigation and philosophical speculation. This has been seen either positively (the speculation is stimulating and helpful) or negatively (the speculation is fruitless and confusing). It is a methodology that alienates angels from your average believer, and not only believers. Many theologians today have now given up trying to understand angels or make them relevant to day-to-day life. Frameworks that are usually used to discuss angels have categories of nature, substance, eternity, knowledge, organisation, speech, fall, and creation. This methodology (explained in chapter 2) presents angels in an abstract and technical way. Angels are distant, obscure, and puzzling. And when angels are not considered so negatively, all too often their mystery—(overly) positively presented—provides a seedbed for all kinds of odd and speculative philosophies and theologies.

However, this is not how the Bible portrays angels. In contrast to the rarefied discussions about them, or the equally rarefied discussions to reject the earlier rarefied discussions, Scripture, in sober and simple terms, with no great elaboration and embellishment, simply describes to us what angels do and have done, with little reference to anything else. We see messages of encouragement, revelation, and guidance; we see judgment and correction; we see strengthening; we see journeying; we see prayer and worship. We see virtually no theological debate or comment about them, and no speculative discussions either. It is a reasonable, restrained, and sober presentation, yet more importantly it is a *practical* depiction; a *pastoral* understanding.

And this made me wonder. Surely the best way to understand angels is to use the framework that Scripture itself provides, and Scripture, while allowing some space for abstract wonderings, focuses far more on what angels practically do and have done. Surely our methodology should reflect this balance and focus. Naturally, speculative investigation has a place within theology. For example, rationalist, post-Enlightenment, Western thought and theology tend to sit uncomfortably with the supernatural, spiritual, and unseen, and so have often struggled with the ancient Jewish worldview of the Bible—where an active unseen realm is taken as read, and so not explained as *we* would want. Thus it natural that, when approached from within this post-Enlightenment milieu, angels inevitably have something of the abstract about them. However, the abstract should not usurp the primary pastoral depiction of Scripture, as it too often has done, and so we should not try to place upon angels a methodology foreign to the biblical revelation, one which loses the pastoral focus. My PhD dealt with all the traditional scholastic categories and the Reformation reactions against these. However, I never thought that this really got to the heart of what angels were all about. These categories not only didn't sit right with me, but didn't seem to with the biblical texts either. For example, the invisible angelic army in 2 Kgs 6 brings comfort in a time of extreme danger, yet does this lead me to consider how angels are organised in heaven? Not really. Or Gabriel's visit to Zechariah in Luke 1, which provides him with a crash course in parenting a prophet. What in that passage draws me to wonder about angelic knowledge? Not very much.

To make the point even clearer: is Paul's call to us to know that "we will judge the angels" (1 Cor 6:3) an exhortation to deepen our understanding of eschatology, or an exhortation to examine our attitudes and motives? Does it invite us to theological exploration, or to an exploration of our own lives, heart, and actions? I think Paul draws us more toward the latter than former, toward the pastoral, as does the broad sweep of the biblical revelation.

It all began to look like a square peg in a round hole, and, after more pondering, I started to ask the question, "*Is the scholastic model the best model for looking at angels, at all?*" Further reflection finally led me, on an Applied Theology course six years after my PhD, to begin to put two and two together, and refine the question to "*Instead of a scholastic framework, would angels be better understood through a pastoral model of theology?*" How would angelology look if the framework one used had categories such as "promoting spiritual wholeness," "personal support," "helping integration into church," or "counselling"? Would it work? The answer to that question is this book, and my answer is "Yes!" I am convinced that the pastoral and relational model is the one which Scripture itself invites us to use, and not to use this model can only lead to a skewed or impoverished view of angels and their ministry.

How does Scripture describe angels to us? Heb 1:14 sums it up neatly: "Are not all angels ministering spirits sent to serve those who will inherit salvation?" Ministry and service to the people of God is the biblical focus. As a personal exercise, whenever you come across angels in the Bible (either in a sermon, personal study, or devotional reading), simply ask yourself, "*How is this passage presenting angels?*" Are they presented theologically or philosophically? Are they presented as mysteries to be explored? Or are they presented as one of God's ways of intervening in human affairs, as a response to a pastoral concern or problem being faced? Going further, how do the angels describe themselves to us? Do any angels in Scripture appear and then, before anything else, say something like: "Behold, I am an immaterial heavenly being of awesome power and mysterious nature, who lives halfway up a celestial hierarchy. My supernatural knowledge has given me insight into your situation." No, they say, for example, "I am Gabriel," or "I am a fellow servant, with you and your brethren, who hold to the testimony of Jesus" (Luke 1:19; Rev 19:10). More often than not they say "*Do not fear!*" to put people at their ease. These are descriptions based in relationship and service and a wish to communicate, not theological or philosophical categories. Angels have names. Angels converse with people. Angels are relational beings who, under God, serve God's people.

ONE PLANK OF MANY: PSALM 91

One criticism of any book that majors on angels, especially from a Christian context, is that it could obscure God, and might, generally, mislead people into worshipping them or over-focussing upon them. Many New Age and some Roman Catholic and Eastern Orthodox devotional resources are often cited as evidence for this possibility. It is a valid point. However, to make very clear where I stand, and where this book will be pitched, I will return to Scripture once again for my framework. Psalm 91 provides us with the perfect context for the book.

The Psalm begins with the wonderful truth that God is a refuge and fortress, in whom we can dwell. We can live in God's (safe) shadow, and find protection and safety under his wings (vv. 1, 2, 4, 9). God will protect those who trust him from those who wish to set traps, from illness, pestilence, and plague (vv. 3, 6), and from threats that come at night. While those who trust may witness others falling, they themselves will not. (v. 7) Verse 10 sums it up saying, "No evil shall befall you." In verse 11, we are then told one of the ways in which God does this: by his angels. But note it is *one* of the ways. The Psalms, and Bible as a whole, are rich with stories of God saving and protecting his people, with not one angel in sight. However, it is nonetheless true that "*He will command His angels concerning you.*" To do what?

- Guard you in all your ways.

- Bear you up lest you strike your foot against a stone.

- Tread and trample upon the lion and adder (serpent).

The Psalm ends (vv. 14–16) with God himself speaking, and he reaffirms who the source of protection is—it is God, and *God alone*. God will protect; answer when people call; help those in trouble; as well as rescuing and honoring them. God will satisfy those who love and trust him, and he will show them his salvation.

So what can we learn from this? The Psalm begins and ends with God as the source and director of salvation and protection. Sandwiched in the middle we get three verses, which indicate angels have a role within this, *under God's command*. The role is wide, dealing with day-to-day activity (*all your ways*), physical protection, and suggests spiritual protection to help defeat evil (perhaps demonic) attack.

This Psalm tells us that angelic ministry, while it might be comprehensive and rich, must start and finish in God. It must never usurp God, or sideline God, or be uprooted out of God, but must always sit within, and beneath, God's wider will, grace, and schemes. Angels sit beneath the shadow of his wings, just as much as we do. They are part of the shadow that God casts which keeps us safe, part of the refuge, part of the safekeeping. They are not that which casts the shadow, nor that in which we find ultimate comfort.

God uses angels as a part of his loving pastoral care toward his creation. God, in sovereign power and wisdom, can act however he chooses. He can answer prayer by acting directly, or by using another human, or by using his angelic ministers. If he chooses to use his angels, he can use them visibly or invisibly. And even if he uses them visibly, we are told that sometimes we don't see or realise it is an angel! For example, God had the choice to either feed Elijah by ravens, or by a widow's generosity, or through a miracle with flour and oil, or by his angel. Different situations elicited different methods of response from God to address the same problem. Four times Elijah was hungry, three times God fed him in ways other than by his angel, but he used his angel nonetheless. And when he did use his angel, Elijah was not only fed but also guided and consoled. Sometimes we need more than our physical hunger sated, but I am getting ahead of myself. Angelic care is but one plank among many, but a wonderful plank nevertheless.

There is one last point I wish to make about my methodology. Many books about angels cite historical examples of angelic ministry, sometimes at the expense of the Scriptural accounts. In contrast, this book will cite no other evidence than that found in Scripture. It is not that I do not believe in angelic ministry today. In fact, during the writing of this book in Oxford, I met two people who had had serious bike accidents, and who, while waiting for the ambulance to arrive, said they experienced the comforting care of an angel, speaking to them and holding them. Angels do meet people in need today, just as they did in biblical times. I do not deny this, but for the purposes of this book I believe the Bible provides more than enough information.

Angels, indeed pastoral angelology, can only find meaning in relationship to God, and as we shall see, this is the Triune God. God has a myriad of ways to enact his will, show his grace, and demonstrate his love within his creation. Angels are but one of these ways, and they are a way that God has consistently cited. Over 270 times angels are mentioned in the Bible, and if you include the references to God's "host," that doubles to nearly 600. The Bible is the revelation of God, which he uses to tell us of his wonderful free gift of salvation. We need to be faithful to Scripture and consider why angels are so often spoken of, and what they have to do with our lives.

1

An Overview of Angelic Ministry in the Bible

A NGELOLOGY HAS BEEN, AT various times during the history of
the church, either deeply engaged with or almost completely ignored, with little time spent on the ground in-between. This tendency
to extreme approaches has led to corrective measures being almost as
excessive. Theologies were built around overreactions, and, eventually,
extreme reactions became the current norm when considering angels.
This means that when one reads about angels, what one sees is generally flowing from an already existing position, which, as we shall see in
chapter 2, is either an extreme position driven by a reaction to another
extreme position, or a simple, almost blind, continuation of what has
gone before.

Polarised and preconceived theological assumptions about angels
strongly shape how people view them and their ministry, and so you,
the reader, need to be as free from preconceived theological assumptions as possible. Although nobody is truly influence-free, it is possible
to minimise our inherent biases, and this is especially important in the
area of angelology where the influences seem to be particularly strong
and deep-seated.

The following biblical survey is brief and simple, introducing the
issues, questions, and mysteries that have traditionally surrounded
angels. I have tried to relay what the Bible says without adding too
much theological comment. However, I have assumed that when symbolic language is used around angels, it is intentional and purposeful,
and designed to be understood by the reader. For example, therefore,
when we read in Rev 8 that angels are involved in presenting prayers to
God, even though the language has a symbolic feel to it, it nevertheless
has the intention to lead the reader to conclude that angels are, somehow, involved in presenting prayer to God, and not to conclude that
they are not. The exact dynamic of the symbolism may need deeper

investigation to understand specifically what it means, but broadly the symbolic language points to what it suggests. Also, for the purposes of this book the term "angel" is used to include *all* the heavenly beings and not simply those that the Bible designates as "angels." So while not directly called "angels," I shall refer to cherubim, seraphim, and the so-called "living creatures," for example, as groups within the angelic society. Thus, in my terminology, biblical angels are a *subdivision* of this wider category of "angels." In later chapters I will add further detail, explaining how specific passages might be interpreted. I also include, in this initial chapter, something about how first century Judaism would have viewed the Old Testament evidence, and so what would have influenced early Christian understanding. However, as we go through the material, you will see that many of the (later) questions customarily asked of the passages are not questions the passages themselves pose. Frustrating though this can be we should not force the content so that questions raised in our minds over-dominate our reading of Scripture. Scripture, itself, should set the agenda.

OLD AND NEW TESTAMENTS

Angelic Creation and Fall

While it is clear that angels are created beings, made by God,[1] evidence is sparse regarding further issues. For example, *when* were angels created? Gen 1:1 talks of the heavens and earth being created, but only the earth was formless and void, which could indicate that the heavens were not, and that angels had been created already. Alternatively, since angels are called beings of light, were they created as a part of *light*?[2]

The existence of demons suggests that some angels fell, but *when* was this? It was presumably before the serpent (which has been traditionally understood to be Satan) tempted Eve in Gen 3, but was it after Gen 1:4, or perhaps after 1:31, since at both these junctures God saw everything as *good* and demons are certainly not good. Why did they fall? The Bible does not tell us. Some scholars have looked at Isa 14:12–15 which, whilst not *directly* about Satan, may be interpreted to *indirectly* suggest that Lucifer wanted to become like God. It was also suggested, in some post-biblical sources, there may have been jealousy on the part of some angels that humans were only lower than the angels for a while,

1. Neh 9:6; cf. Ps 148:2–5; Col 1:16.
2. Gen 1:3; cf. Heb 1:7; Ezek 1:13–14; 2 Cor 11:14.

and later God was going to exalt humans above angels via the honor of the Incarnation. And once in this exalted position humans would judge the angels. This anticipated reversal of fortunes and status led Satan and then the other demons to fall, and this is the source of their hatred of both God and humanity.[3] However, little is clear cut as to exactly how and why the angelic fall happened.

Angelic Nature

Angels are described as beings of light, fire, and wind (or spirit), but none of these descriptions really say as much as one would like.[4] Angels are spatially limited, so they cannot be in more than one place at one time,[5] and it is possible that a large number of angels or demons can inhabit a relatively small space.[6] Angels are intelligent, holy, and obey the will of God,[7] and are able to exercise moral judgement since some, as we have seen, misused that faculty and sinned, and are now subject to judgement.[8] The fact they are described as holy, by implication, says that they are without sin. However, the idea of them being sinless raises questions when faced with a couple of enigmatic verses—Job 4:18 talks of angels being charged with folly (error), and Col 1:20 talks of all things in heaven (which presumably includes the angelic realm, cf. Col 2:8, 18) needing reconciliation through Christ. How does one balance angels being sinless, yet with folly, and needing reconciliation with God? This again raises the question as to how holy and sinless beings could fall, and why those who didn't fall now don't, and those who fell now can't be reconciled.

The nature of the angels is of importance since men *will be like unto, or equal to, angels in the resurrection.*[9] This state of being *isangelloi* (ισαγγελοι: *like the angels*), while in the immediate context of the verse primarily relates to marriage relationships, might also be further understood in terms of the nature of an angelic body, and/or morally, spiritually and intellectually, and/or immortality, but it is not detailed.

3. Ps 8:5–6; Heb 2:7; 1 Cor 6:3 cf. Rev 12:1–9.

4. Ezek 1:13; Heb 1:7; Matt 28:3.

5. Dan 10:13.

6. Luke 8:30.

7. Matt 25:31; Job 5:1; Dan 8:13; Ps 103:20–21.

8. 2 Pet 2:4; Jude 6; 1 Cor 6:3.

9. Luke 20:36; cf. Matt 22:30.

Angels in heaven do not marry, but arguably do have gender and perhaps, as fallen angels, might be able to engage in sexual intercourse.[10] However, as previously mentioned, humans will be exalted above the angels,[11] which could also have implications for what is understood by humans being *isangelloi.*

Although angels are spirit beings, they can appear to humans in physical form. People do not always see them, and sometimes need God to illuminate their minds in order to do so.[12] They usually take human form (the main exception being when they appear as *living creatures*), and can be mistaken simply for other humans.[13] The angelic appearances can also come with a brilliant light or a glory, which could be either them reflecting the *glory of the Lord,* or it could be a glory or shining of their own being. [14]

Angelic Organisation

Angels, in the wider sense of heavenly creatures, have many names in the Bible, and come in a number of "species"—angels, archangels, living creatures, seraphim, and cherubim.[15] Heavenly beings also appear to be referred to as sons of God, holy ones, spirits, watchers, thrones, rulers, dominions, principalities, and powers.[16] These names may indicate different groupings within the angelic realm, but what the groups are and how they interrelate is not made clear. In addition to this, some have personal names ascribed to them. Michael and Gabriel are the only two mentioned in the Bible, but other angels are named in apocryphal literature.[17] In heaven, angels are also called an army or a host, and the size of this host varies from twelve legions, to myriads and thousands, but these are probably symbolic for very large numbers.[18] Angels are pictured as forming a choir who serve at God's throne, singing, playing

10. Matt 22:30; Zech 5:9; Gen 6:1ff.

11. Heb 2:7.

12. Num 22:22ff. esp. v. 31; 2 Kgs 6:17; Heb 13:2.

13. Gen 18:16; Judg 13:6; cf. Ezek 1:4ff.

14. Matt 28:3; Ezek 1:13 cf. Matt 16:27.

15. Rev 5:11; 4:7; Isa 6:2–6; Gen 3:24; Ezek 1:4ff.

16. Job 1:6; Ps 89:5–7; Heb 1:14; Dan 4:13; Col 1:16; Eph 1:21.

17. Dan 10:13; Rev 12:7; Luke 1:19.

18. Matt 26:53; Rev 5:11; Heb 12:22; Deut 33:2.

instruments, and using censers.[19] They are also called a court, which stand round God's throne and sing praises to him, converse with him,[20] and perhaps have a level of influence too.[21] As with human courts there seem to be different roles, ranks, and levels of authority assigned to different angels—the simple fact that there are angels and *arch*angels indicates a hierarchical organisation, all of which is under Christ's authority.[22]

Angelic Knowledge

Angels have vast knowledge, beyond that of humans, but limited by God.[23] They have an undefined form of speech and language, but can speak the various languages of humankind, and they can discern between good and evil.[24] Angels desire to know more of God, and it is through the church here on earth, that God enables them to learn more of himself.[25]

Angelic Ministry

Angels take a great interest in the affairs of humanity, and because of this want to operate within the earthly realm, blessing and protecting people. This was true regarding Jesus, and angels were with him throughout his earthly life—his conception and birth, his adult life, his death, his resurrection, and his ascension.[26] In addition, after the ascension of Christ, angelic activity did not cease and angels continued to interact with the fledgling church.[27] The letters and epistles to the early church testified to the work of angels, the clearest statement being Heb 1:14: "Are not all angels ministering servants sent to serve those who will inherit salvation?"

The question arises here whether angels minister solely to the faithful, or to all people irrelevant of their beliefs, in order to lead them closer

---

19. Rev 5:9; 14:3; 15:3 cf. Isa 6; Luke 2:13ff.
20. Rev 7:11; Job 1:6; Ps 89:7.
21. cf. 1 Kgs 22:19ff.; Jer 23:18–22; Luke 12:8–9.
22. Eph 1:20; 3:10; 1 Pet 3:22.
23. Matt 24:36.
24. 1 Cor 13:1; 2 Sam 14:17.
25. 1 Pet 1:12; Eph 3:10.
26. Jesus and angels will discussed in depth in ch. 4.
27. Acts 5:18–20; 8:26–29; 10:3–8; 12:6–11; 27:23–25.

to God. Nonetheless, angelic ministry, whatever its range or limits, is stated to be real and on-going.

Angels observe humans and rejoice when they repent and turn to God, and they also come in response to prayer.[28] It is therefore no surprise the Bible describes a range of instances where angels act within creation, and interact with people. Angels are powerful beings, able to do mighty acts and they follow their mission through to its conclusion.[29] They bring messages to humans from God, and communication can be via dreams,[30] when the recipient is fully alert,[31] or by an audible voice spoken from heaven.[32] These are not necessarily one-way conversations, and people can talk with and question angels.[33]

Angels are also shown to accomplish a range of physical tasks, such as rolling away the stone from Christ's tomb, shutting the mouths of the lions when Daniel was in the den, and freeing people from prison.[34] They protect people on journeys,[35] provide physical assistance,[36] and can perform what are called *psychical* actions where they can *give strength to* people, which may also be indicated by their involvement in healings.[37] Wicked angels, in the form of demons, can strongly influence humans, and this allows the possibility that a good influence may be exerted by a good angel.[38] Again, the opposite side of protection is also shown where angels are portrayed as those who execute God's wrath on earth, and will be involved in the Second Coming of Christ.[39]

In an enigmatic reference in Gen 48:16, an angel is said to have *redeemed* Jacob from *all evil*; whether that means salvation or protection or something else is not clear. One answer could see it as referring to the *Angel of the Lord*, who, at times, is identified with God because

28. Luke 15:10; Dan 10:12–13.

29. 2 Sam 24:16 cf. 2 Pet 2:11; Matt 28:2; Ps 35:5ff.

30. Matt 1:20; 2:13; Gen 31:11.

31. Luke 1:11; 2:9–11; Matt 28:2–7; Mark 16:5–7; Luke 24:4.

32. John 12:29.

33. Luke 1:26–38.

34. Matt 28:2; Dan 6:22; Acts 12:6ff.

35. Gen 16:7 cf. 24:7.

36. Matt 4:11.

37. Luke 22:43; John 5:3–4.

38. Luke 8:30.

39. 2 Sam 24:16; Gen 3:24; 2 Thess 1:5–10; 1 Cor 10:10.

he is worshipped, and that when he speaks his words are attributed to God himself; indeed he is sometimes even identified *as* God. However, elsewhere, the Angel of the Lord is clearly just an angel, so the question remains.[40] This will be examined in more detail in chapter 4. Angels are said to pray for God's people and present their prayers to God, which raises questions around what role angels may have in mediating between God and humans, and how people should respond to this.[41] Throughout the Bible angels are shown to guide and protect, and the idea has developed that people have their own guardian angels. Some passages indicate an individualised ministry by using the pronouns *his* or *their* angel, but these terms are only clearly used in Acts 12:15 and Matt 18:10. [42] This idea, however, could further be supported by indications of the closeness of angels and humans as a single heavenly society, and that both are called *elect*.[43] Further, Rev 1:20 talks of the seven churches having seven angels, and Michael is said to have a special role protecting Israel, which could be developed into there being guardian angels for churches and nations.[44] However, it is also argued that this protection is general and does not demand a specific angel for a specific person/situation. An angel will come and help as God promises, but it might simply be the nearest one at hand!

And just as angels are involved in our lives, so they are in death too. In Jude 9 Michael fought with Satan over the body of Moses, and in Luke 16:22 poor Lazarus was carried to Abraham's side by angels. If one does not die before the Second Coming, then one will still witness angels in action, blowing the trumpet of God, and assisting Christ, helping him with the reaping and gathering, the separation of the wheat and the chaff, and weeding out evil-doers.[45]

Warnings about Angels

Despite all these amazing aspects to angelic ministry, there are very occasionally some warnings about angels, and they fall into two broad

---

40. Gen 16:10–13; Gen 31:11–13; 2 Sam 24:16; Zech 1:11–13.

41. Rev 8:3–4.

42. cf. Ps 34:7, 91:11.

43. Heb 12:22; Rom 11:7; 1 Tim 5:21.

44. Dan 12:1; Jude 9; 1 Thess 4:16.

45. 1 Thess 4:16; 2 Thess 1:7; Matt 24:31; Matt 13:41; Rev 14:14–20.

categories. First, one must not worship them for this places them in the position that only God holds. Second, one cannot always trust angelic visitations, for demons can masquerade as angels and can lie and teach false doctrine.[46]

THE APOCRYPHA

While in Protestant circles the Apocrypha is not considered Scripture, it has exerted a level of influence on angelology over the centuries especially in Roman Catholic and Eastern Orthodox circles. I do not base any arguments on Apocryphal stories in the main sections of the book, sticking squarely to the Old and New Testaments. However, I merely note what it says for the sake of completeness and to recognise its influence in many Christian traditions. Generally, the Apocrypha follows the same lines as the Old Testament, but elaboration and development is evident, some of which appears in the New Testament.

Angels are a vast host gathered before God, where they wait to do his will, and be sent into the world in the form of wind and fire.[47] There is a distinction between good and bad angels, and good angels chase and bind demons.[48] Angels praise and bless God, and encourage people to do the same.[49] Along with God, they see our sins, and our actions cannot be hidden from their gaze.[50]

There are seven holy angels (archangels), one of whom one is Raphael, another Uriel, and another Jeremiel.[51] These angels go into the presence of God and present peoples' prayers to him.[52] They are also sent from heaven in response to prayer to provide assistance and protection.[53] For instance, an angel accompanied Tobias on a journey in order to protect him.[54] Angels can also take on human form, but we cannot recognise them, although the main clue is that angels are not able to eat or drink

---

46. Col 2:18; Rev 19:10; 2 Cor 11:14.

47. 2 Esd 6:3; 2 Esd 8:21–22.

48. Tob 5:21; 2 Mac 11:6; Tob 8:3.

49. Tob 12:6ff.

50. 2 Esd 16:66.

51. 2 Esd 4:1; 4:36.

52. Tob 12:11–15.

53. 2 Mac 11:6; 15:22–23; Bel 33–39.

54. Tobit 5:16–21.

human food.[55] Angels also carry out the sentence or vengeance of God, in both a collective context (upon nations), and also on individual lives, exacting specific punishments.[56]

Angels communicate with humans in a number of ways, such as the apocalyptic visions of 2 Esdras where an angel reveals events and visions to Ezra. Ezra is also reprimanded and taught by an angel.[57] Angels are shown to have great insight into the ways and will of God, but are not told all things and have limits upon their knowledge.[58] Angels are also shown to have certain powers, such a healing and a psychical ability to give strength to people.[59]

WHAT IS THE MINISTRY OF ANGELS BEYOND THE NEW TESTAMENT PERIOD?

The brief synopsis of the biblical data about angels, while fascinating, gives us a tantalising lack of specific detail. So how are we to interpret it? What is the framework we are to use to understand it? Much of this overview has tried to simply note what texts say, though I am aware that the way in which they were interpreted in the later Christian tradition has inevitably informed my reading. However, when it comes to making sense of biblical texts about angels, what is more significant than later Christian traditions is an understanding of the beliefs about angels alive in first century Judaism—the seed bed in which early Christianity and the New Testament texts grew. Which aspects of those beliefs were kept, which were rejected, and what was new to the fledgling movement?

It is worth noting that the Second Temple period (which ran from around 516 BC through the period when Christ lived and ended in 70 AD), "witnessed a fundamental change . . . and the importance of angels [grew]."[60] By the first century, angels were thought of as named, personal beings, understood to be organised hierarchically, and seen as guardians over people and nations; this last idea being well established by Christ's

---

55. Tob 5 (esp. v. 21); Tob 12:19.

56. Sir 48:21; 1 Mac 7:41; Sus 55–59.

57. 2 Esd 2:44ff.; 4:1ff.; 7:1.

58. 2 Esd 5:31–32; 4:52.

59. Tob 3:16–17; 2 Esd 5:15.

60. Flusser and Yadin, *Judaism of the Second Temple Period*, 40.

time.[61] In fact, according to 1 Enoch 39:12, the whole earth is full of spirits (i.e., angels).[62] Thus many first-century Jews believed in angels as powerful beings who served God, in a council around his throne.[63] While it is popularly thought that Sadducees totally rejected the concept of angels (c.f. Acts 23:8), this is not fully clear, and it is possible that what they actually rejected was the *highly-developed* angelology of other Jews in this period—such as the common belief in guardian angels being responsible for the fate of individuals and nations, and about people becoming *isangelloi* in the resurrection.[64]

The world being full of spirits also included evil spirits and demons. It was widely accepted that the devil was responsible for sickness and sin, and angels were those who fought the devil and his schemes. Tobit is one of the first books to spell this out.[65] In Tobit, the angel Raphael bound demons and healed the sick, but by the first century there was a strong tradition found the Book of Enoch saying that Raphael would repair and heal not only individual lives, but the damage caused on the whole earth by the devil and evil magic. In other traditions angels gave wisdom and taught Noah and Solomon about healing medicines.[66] Simply put, angels had wide-ranging influence over lives, and were a means by which demons were conquered. Therefore one needed to understand them well for one's life to be peaceful.[67]

In this light, it is no surprise that groups like the Essenes had well developed angelologies, seeing an exemplary harmony between the heavenly and temporal order: even the company of angels and the course of heavenly worship were organised on hieratic lines. Their worship was set to heaven's calendar, a calendar which angels (holy ones) not only observed and obeyed, but gave.[68] The unity of the (Essene) human and angelic community (in the here and now, not only in the future) was

---

61. Hannah, *Michael and Christ*, 125.

62. Flusser and Yadin, *Judaism of the Second Temple Period*, 40–41.

63. *Cambridge History Of Judaism*, Vol. 3, 92; Harbury, *Jewish Messianism* 120.

64. *Cambridge History of Judaism*, Vol. 3, 441–42; cf. *2 Bar.* 51:10; *1 En.* 103:4; Harbury, *Jewish Messianism*, 120; cf. Davidson, *Angels at Qumran*, 155, 200, 283, 284.

65. Vermes, *Jesus The Jew*, 61; *Cambridge History of Judaism*, Vol. 2, 47.

66. Vermes, *Jesus The Jew*, 62; cf. *1 En.* 10:4–8;7:1; 8:3.

67. So powerful and reverenced were the angels that some even thought the Messiah would be an angelic figure. Harbury, *Jewish Messianism*, 86–87, 90–91, 105.

68. *Cambridge History of Judaism* Vol. 3, 451–52, 60; Davidson, *Angels at Qumran*, 91–92.

central, and so right conduct was vital.[69] Angels were literally present in the worshipping congregation, and here heaven and earth met in a true and real way—*the praying community on earth joined with the angels in heaven to worship.*[70]

Josephus also underlined another reason why this understanding of angels was so important. The origin of evil was to be found not so much in the fall of Adam but in Gen 6, when the sons of God and the women of earth had sexual relations, and their offspring (the nephilim) became demons.[71] This fall created two kingdoms—one of good angels, led by Michael (Prince of Light), serving God, and the other being the realm of demons, led by the devil (Angel of Darkness). And while they battled for human "souls" on earth now, later there would be one final, eschatological battle between the two realms.

Angelic pronouncements were common in apocalyptic thought, and the idea that they revealed mysteries and secrets to seers (either through dreams or visions, or taking the seer into heaven) was common.[72] And this is not surprising as angels were thought by some to have not only dictated the Torah to Moses, but also the later book of Jubilees.[73] Good Jews would be confessed as such by God, before the angels,[74] and angels interceded for humans.[75] Thus the invocation of, reverence of, and honor of angels—in prayer and hymns—was a normal part of much popular Jewish piety.[76]

So angels, around the time of Christ, were understood as beings involved in the day to day life of believers, as their guardians, who could drive away demonic oppression and sickness, who protected and prayed for the faithful, and gave wisdom, knowledge, and guidance from God. Angels were also a part of one's devotional life, and an awareness of their realm and worship was important for one's own life. To put it simply, angels were understood to have, amongst other things, an essentially pastoral role toward God's people, in the most practical of ways.

69. Davidson, *Angels at Qumran*, 166–70, 316–19.

70. *The Oxford Bible Commentary*, 803.

71. *Cambridge History of Judaism*, Vol. 3, 463–64; See J.W. 2:142; cf. *Jub.* 7:21ff.

72. Ibid., 780, 782, 787.

73. Ibid. Vol. 2, 433.

74. Vermes, *Jesus the Jew*, 195; *Jub.* 1:24–25.

75. Davidson, *Angels at Qumran*, 54–57.

76. Harbury, *Jewish Messianism*, 121.

Sadly, despite this enlightening background, which finds clear echoes throughout early Christian writings, the New Testament does not then give us a plain guide in "How, as Christians, to understand angels," but it does give us pointers with which we can work. Some theologies make little distinction between the biblical evidence of the Old Testament (including the Apocrypha), the Gospels, and the rest of the New Testament. However, with the giving of the Holy Spirit at Pentecost, a whole new framework is placed upon the table for the people of God. Does this still include the ministry of angels? If so, has the angelic role changed at all? What do angels do post-Pentecost now the Holy Spirit is given, since if angelic ministry radically changes pre- and post-Pentecost then simple reference back into the Old Testament and the Gospels would be an inadequate framework to use.

The Book of Acts tells the story of the post-Pentecost early church, and in it angels are still clearly active. Richer exposition of the passages (including the epistles) will be found later in this book, but for now one can reference an angel freeing apostles from jail (5:19; 12:7), another encouraging the apostles to continue to preach in the temple after persecution (5:19–20), another telling Philip to go to the Ethiopian eunuch (8:26). Yet another is instrumental in bringing the gospel to the Gentiles (10:3–7), a further one kills Herod (12:23), and finally an angel assures Paul he will get to Rome (27:23). Here are clear roles of protection and judgment, guidance and assurance, and a wish to advance the gospel and the church of God. Although these roles have parallels in the Old Testament and contemporary presentations of angels, one cannot simply claim that the evidence in Acts is comprehensive in its scope and is detailed enough for us to say *all* Old Testament descriptions and contemporary understandings of angelic ministry remain on the table. For example, would one need angels to be special bearers of God's presence to his people and others, now the Holy Spirit lives within believers, and stirs non-Christians toward Christ? Yet consider Cornelius, who was initially met by an angel, not the Spirit, though he was filled with the Spirit at a later stage. We have evidence of angelic ministry continuing in the early church, but little specific framework, and questions remain.

Thankfully, though, the rest of the New Testament does not leave us totally without guidance, and in one place in particular we have a pointer as to how we are to understand angelic ministry post-Pentecost. The verse is Heb 1:14 and this will underpin much of what follows. It is by no means the be-all-and-end-all of the biblical evidence for the post-Pentecost ministry of angels, however, it is well worth looking at the verse and its context in some depth to see how rich the New Testament's, and in fact the whole Bible's, understanding of angelic ministry is and continues to be.

Hebrews 1:14

The book of Hebrews was written to Jewish Christians, almost certainly prior to Nero's persecution in the mid 60s AD and the destruction of the Temple in 70 AD. Heb 1 is an extended discussion of how Christ is superior to the angels. As we have seen, in Jewish thought and theology, angels had a special place, not only due to the amazing ministry wrought by them throughout the whole Old Testament, but that it was the angels who gave the Law to the Israelites (Acts 7:53; Gal 3:19; Heb 2:2) and angels that influenced much of day to day life. The thrust of the argument is that if the Jews listened to angels, *how much more* should they listen to Jesus? So, Heb 1 sets the scene, saying that not only are the angels below Christ, but that Christ is the perfect revelation of God himself, and indeed is God. Therefore the angels serve him, worship him, and everything else that follows from being a creature made by the one Creator.

The place of the angels is plain, and the writer sets them firmly in their place below Christ as the Son of God, who is God. However, the writer does not follow this line of thought through to a point where this means that angels are now redundant. As Guthrie writes: "The writer [of Hebrews] is certainly not wishing to belittle the function of angels . . . What is important at the moment (of the writing of the letter) is to observe that heavenly messengers are occupied in a ministry directed toward the salvation of men."[77] So, angels are still active post-Pentecost, yet what is their place now? Guthrie has already given us a hint, but their place is properly described in verse 14: "Are they not all ministering spirits, sent out to render service for the sake of those who will inherit salvation?" This is a verse which one can skim over quickly, and miss the real and deep import. An examination of the Greek behind the English is instructive in pulling out its riches.

77. Guthrie, *Hebrews*, 79.

"Ουχι παντες εισιν λειτουργικα πνευματα ει διακονιαν αποστελ-λομενα δια τους μελλοντας κληρονομειν σωτηριαν." What does "ministering" (Gk. *leitourgika* / λειτουργικα) suggest? This is the only use of the word in the New Testament. The exact use of this form of verb in Greek is unusual, and other contemporary occurrences (beyond the Bible) shed little light on its use here. Therefore, direct comparison with other contexts to find out more about what it may mean, is not easy. Although the root meaning of public and religious service echoes into other words and other verses, if the writer simply wanted to say that "angels minister," he could have easily used *leitourgia* / λειτουργια (note the "k" at the end is gone), a word he uses in other places in the epistle. The fact that he does not use it here suggests he wants to say something other than simple ministering—he wants to make a point. For example, Heb 10:11 uses a term similar to *leitourgia* to mean officiate as a priest, Acts 13:2 for ministering in the church (for God, to people), and Rom 15:27 has a usage which is potentially as rich as to mean to minister, to assist, and to provide succor. Yet these words are not *leitourgika*. These other references speak of humans as priests, and Christ as *the* High Priest, but here it is something else. The construction of the word points to the idea that while angels are not priests (as humans can be, and Christ ultimately is), nevertheless they have a function within a priestly context. The function associated with this word, while not described in the New Testament, is found in the Greek translation of the Old Testament (LXX), with which the readers of Hebrews would have been familiar, and it is probable in this context that the writer wanted to echo the LXX.[78]

The word occurs only six times in the LXX, and each time it paints an interesting picture. Exod 31:10 and 39:1 use the term to speak of Aaron's special robes of *ministry* which he was to wear, when *serving* in the tabernacle. Num 4:12 applies it to "all the *instruments of service* with which they minister in the sanctuary." Similarly Num 4:26 uses it for "*vessels of service* which they minister with." Num 7:5 applies it to the gifts that the prince of Israel gave to the LORD which were for the *service of the tabernacle* and used by the priests. Finally, 2 Chr 24:14 applies it to "*vessels for the house* of the LORD, vessels for whole burnt offerings." Where the echo in these passages takes us is clear. Ellingworth

---

78. The word has only one other ancient attestation. The Jewish writer Philo uses *leitourgika* in the context of the Song of Moses (Deut 32–33), and said that the ministering angels would enjoy the beauty of the song and worship (*Virtues* 78).

says: "The LXX use of λειτουργικα is overwhelmingly cultic."[79] Similarly Strathmann says, "It always bears a sacral sense, belonging to the cultus, with reference to the vessels and instruments."[80] Yet the word is not only cultic. A historical study of the word in Rabbinic Judaism suggests that during the late first century (just after Hebrews was written, to an audience who would probably have been aware of trends that shaped the plant that would grow into rabbinic Judaism) it may have gained a meaning more than simple service—a meaning with clear ethical and spiritual content.[81]

Thus, while one cannot know exactly why the writer to the Hebrews used the word, his use of it indicates he wanted to make a specific point. He would have known both the LXX and, more than likely, the proto-Rabbinic backgrounds to the word, as well as the rich understanding that surrounded angels at the time, and so must have used it knowingly and specifically to an audience who also understood them.

Therefore, *leitourgika* indicates special sacred vessels or instruments, used by the priests, in the temple (including the sanctuary) for the priestly service of God, which includes the sacrifices and offerings. Angels are not priests, this is clear. Yet they are priestly, and they have a role which is not only plain service, but one with possible ethical and spiritual overtones too. And to maybe push this further, one might reflect that while a direct comparison is probably not possible, the wider context of Hebrews, with Jesus as the one true High Priest who made the one true sacrifice, means the use of the word echoes the suggestion that angels are priestly vessels of service used by our High Priest, Jesus Christ, for those who will inherit salvation—for the church.

The structure of Hebrews indicates this idea. The book starts by setting angels in their place as servants of Christ for the church (1:14). In the central section of the book, angels are not mentioned because its focus, after priesthood and covenant, is sacrifice and atonement, which is the sole role of Christ (Heb 3–10). Once the atonement is made, and Christians appropriate this through conversion, one then needs to live the Christian life. You then get the classic chapter of faith (11) followed by chapters 12 and 13 on living the Christian life. In this final section, angels reappear in a vision of the heavenly city and of life lived with the

79. Ellingworth *Hebrews*, 132.

80. *TDNT.* Vol. 4, 231.

81. R. Meyer in *TDNT.* Vol. 4, 225.

angels (12:22–24, cf. 13:14). Angels also arise in 13:2 in which readers are encouraged to be hospitable towards strangers in case one is entertaining angels without knowing it. The knowledge of angels serving in heaven and working on earth is part of the instructions on living the Christian life. Christians are to be aware of angels rendering service for those who will inherit salvation. So what exactly is that service offered? It is described in the Greek of Heb 1:14 as *diakonian* (διακονιαν). The word (and close variants) occurs thirty-four times in the New Testament, and its use is varied, all occasions having the meaning of forms of service and ministry. It can have the meaning of simple day-to-day hard work. So in Luke 10:40 it is the work that Martha did around the house, while Mary was at Jesus' feet; and in Acts 6:1 it describes the serving of food to widows. However, it also has the wider meaning of spiritual ministry as opposed to simple physical assistance and support. Acts 1:17 (cf. 1:25) says that the apostle to replace Judas would share in the *ministry* of the twelve, and Acts 6:4 tells us that apostolic ministry was a *ministry* of the word as opposed to the waiting on tables.

This ministerial aspect is further developed in other passages. For example, Acts 12:25 (cf. Acts 11:29) uses it to describe the mission undertaken by Paul and Barnabas to Jerusalem, with the gift to help the church through the famine. While this was a predominantly humanitarian act, would they merely have gone and handed over the cash and left, or would there also have been some preaching, prayer, and personal ministry too? (Cf. 2 Cor 8:4; 9:1, 12, 13; 11:8.) In fact, in Acts 20:24 (cf. 21:19) it is the *ministry* Paul received from the Lord Jesus. This is echoed in 1 Tim 1:12 where God puts Paul into his *service*, which flows straight into Rom 11:13, where Paul makes much of his *ministry* to the Gentiles, and Rom 12:7 where it is the ministry of serving in the church (cf. 1 Cor 12:5). It is a service and ministry to Christians (1 Cor 16:15), received through God's mercy (2 Cor 4:1), that is not to be discredited (2 Cor 6:3). More pointedly, from a pastoral perspective, it is the ministry of reconciliation (2 Cor 5:18). It is a ministry one is called to discharge, and to be done diligently (2 Tim 4:5). Further, it is an individual's ministry received in the Lord (Col 4:17), to equip Christians for works of service/ministry (Eph 4:12). This is a ministry which is worked out corporately, for example where Mark is useful to Paul's ministry (2 Tim 4:11).

One could argue it is not necessary to give such a meaning to *diakonian*, and say it only means manual service as shown in Acts 6:1 and

Luke 10:40. However, within the context of Heb 1 and the epistle as a whole (which speaks of priestly service and the service of the temple), and how the average Greek-speaking Jew would have read this, to limit the word in that manner does not do justice to the wider evidence or context. Mirroring the priestly, ethical and spiritual dimensions of *leito-urgika*, *diakonian* has an echo directly into the wide and rich ministry one would see in God's church.

The next part of the verse answers the question, *For whom, specifically, is this ministry?* The phrase κληρονομειν σωτηριαν / *klēronomein sōtērian* translates as "those who will inherit salvation," but what does this mean? In technical terms *klēronomein* (to inherit) is, in Greek, a present, infinitive, active, which means it is describing an event which is both present and also on-going. It means *those who currently are, and those who later will also inherit*. It is not a one-off event, nor an event of limited duration, but is currently active and will continue to be into the future. What is this on-going inheritance? In context of Heb 6:12 (inherit) and 11:7 (heir) it is the inheritance of salvation, and this is reflected directly in Matt 25:34, Mark 10:17, and Titus 3:7.

As for *sōtērian*, it means salvation. Some commentators try to suggest that the salvation here is simply describing help in the present, and not the eternal salvation which God promises through Christ, once again limiting the role of angels to simple physical assistance. However, even a cursory examination of the use of the word in Hebrews (2:3; 5:9; 9:28) and the wider New Testament (e.g., Rom 11:14; 1 Cor 1:21) shows how this does no justice to the word and its context. This phrase, then, means Christians (the body of Christ), who will inherit the salvation of God that is found through Christ.

While this may seem a long-winded explanation, it is important since it sets the basic tone for the rest of this book. Leaving aside those who argue that angelic ministry has ceased and so this verse cannot mean what it seems to say, some want to limit the ministry of angels to physical help and protection in times of trouble alone. Others still may want to read this as something deeply spiritual and personal, almost autonomous of God, and so develop an understanding of angelic ministry to rich, even epic, proportions. The words and their application here, however, reject such simple and narrow classifications, and these extremes of thought. The verse highlights the difference and the similarity of the mission of angels and of humans—the heavenly source and the earthly outworking. The service, directed to and for the glory of God, is both physical and practical (external), with a spiritual and ethical aspect to it (internal). It is within and outside the church, and has an element of calling and compulsion by God to perform it.

This verse does not suggest a limitation on angelic ministry, but the tenses and shape of the Greek speak of an on-going ministry and work of the angels toward the people of God. Their ministry cannot be divorced from the work of Christ, and will always point there. So what is that ministry and what does that look like? Heb 1:14 points directly to where we need to go, since in a more expanded form (taking into account the wider context of Hebrews and the New Testament use of the individual words) we could paraphrase the verse as follows:

> Are not angels, special, sacred priestly vessels, set apart for holy use, used by the one High Priest and God, Jesus Christ, to serve and minister to, physically and spiritually, those, who through salvation wrought by Christ alone, are in his church now, and those who will be brought into his church in times to come?

This looks like a very wordy, over-amplified explanation of the verse, but it is crucial to understand fully what it says. The whole of the Old Testament ministry is still on the table, as the Jewish Christians reading this would have instantly recognised, but this ministry is now directed toward the growth of the church of Jesus Christ. As my next chapter will show, this practical ministry of angels is often minimised by many theological traditions, in favour of more speculative wonderings. Yet when time is spent on the biblical background, in contrast to much of the theology over the past 2000 years, which seems to have just clouded the issue, its abundant richness, rootedness, and basic simplicity, becomes clear.

2

FROM BIBLICAL TIMES UNTIL TODAY

A History of Angelology

THROUGHOUT THE FIRST 1,500 years of Church History, trying to understanding angels and the angelic realm was a recurring pre-occupation, with every detail that could be unearthed in Scripture expounded and added to until comprehensive systems of doctrine were developed. The Reformation and subsequent Enlightenment reacted against this, reactions we still see today in various guises. The pastoral presentation of the Bible was increasingly replaced by technical, philosophical, and speculative theological explorations, clouding the practical simplicity of what was originally presented.[1]

THE FIRST MILLENNIUM

The Christian world/heaven-view grew directly out of the Jewish understanding of the universe, and straight into a Greek philosophical milieu. These two influences—sometimes interacting positively, and other times clashing violently—shaped how angels were viewed.[2] The first to try and synthesise the two was Philo (d. 45 AD), a Jewish Platonist, who conceived the universe in similar terms to Jacob's Ladder (Gen 28).[3] God was at the top, the earth at the bottom, and angels filled the space between. In Philo we see seeds of what was to follow in Christian theology and devotion—God at the top of a ladder or hierarchy, mankind at the bottom, and angels working as intermediaries in the middle.

This idea was further reinforced by the influence of Neo-Platonism, which posited a single source—God—from which all existence

---

1. Much of this chapter from: Macy, *Angels (1547–1662)*, chs. 2–9.

2. Lane, *Unseen*, 3.

3. Plato, *Somn.*, 148, cited in Lane, *Unseen*, 3.

emanates, and to which an individual soul can be mystically united. The universe is fundamentally hierarchical, with gradations of being and nature—the highest being the pure spirit being, which is God, and the lowest the fleshy physical world of humanity. Man reaches God by climbing the hierarchy through mystical experience. God reaches man by being mediated down through the hierarchy.[4] While other features of Neo-Platonism were heavily criticised by Christian theologians, the hierarchical aspect of it was influential.

Numerous early Church (Patristic) theologians wrote about angels.[5] Common themes were their nature, creation, how they fell, what demons are, their knowledge and organisation. Western Christendom, as epitomised by Augustine (354–430), though, was less enamoured with speculative angelology. Augustine derived his limits of angelology from Scripture, as opposed to relying on contemporary philosophy. His christocentric focus allied with a dislike of speculation around angels meant that practical expositions of angelic ministry were far from his mind. In eastern Christendom, however, Augustine was less of an authority and Neo-Platonism retained a stronger influence. How the angels were grouped and organised in heaven was a focus of much discussion, and the idea of a hierarchy down which God mediated himself was developed.[6] Angels led the human soul to Christ, preparing it for its journey toward God. The soul went from transformation to transformation until it reached God. Angels assisted by protecting and promoting a godly life, and helping to purify, to illuminate, and to unify. This was achieved by the angels being a part of the hierarchy down through which God passed his blessing and salvation. The end result of purification and illumination was ascension upward, to unification with Christ, and angels accompanied men on that journey. This basic concept of angelic hierarchy was common, but it was the refined vision proposed by Pseudo Dionysius (c. sixth century) in his *Celestial Hierarchy* that would dominate until the Reformation. Beginning with God, the hierarchy was ordered in three groups of three:

1. Cherubim; Seraphim; Holy Thrones.

2. Powers; Dominions; Authorities.

3. Principalities; Archangels; Angels.

4. Wakefield, *Spirituality*, 275; Louth, *Denys*, 13.

5. A good introduction to this period is Daniélou, *The Angels and their Mission.*

6. Louth, *Denys*, 36–37.

Only the lowest of these ("angels") interacted upon the earth, and it is noteworthy that there is no doctrine of guardian angels in Pseudo Dionysius's model.

Broadly speaking, it is here that Eastern Orthodox angelology finds its focal point. Since this time, it has remained mainly unchanged, marrying a strong doctrine of guardian angels with the Dionysian hierarchy, and this can be found in both popular[7] and theological writings.[8] In the West, however, Christendom had the further threefold impact of Scholasticism, Reformation, and Enlightenment to shape its angelology, and it is to this we now turn.

THE MEDIEVAL PERIOD

Thomas Aquinas and Scholastics
(Twelfth and Thirteenth Centuries)

The medieval period was characterised by intense examination of Patristic angelology. Writings were scrutinised and ideas defined until basic agreement was found around all major issues.[9] Medieval angelology followed well-worn patterns, and Peter Lombard's (d. 1160) *Sentences* set the baseline for how one would use Scripture and understand the Patristic heritage.[10] Most issues came down to one of two or three possible positions, all of which were theologically credible and held by reputable thinkers.[11] Thomas Aquinas (1225–1274) further refined Lombard's position, with his presentation lasting unchallenged until the Reformation.[12] He maintained the Patristic line on the vast majority of questions, while at the same time going to new levels of investigation. He also affirmed the Pseudo Dionysian hierarchies, but explicitly added guardian angels into the system. However what is more instructive is to

---

7. Mother Alexandra, *Holy Angels*.

8. Bulgakov, *The Orthodox Church*, 126–28; Bulgakov, *Jacob's Ladder*; Lossky, *Mystical Theology*, 100–102, 108, 116; Ware, *Orthodox Way*, 62–63; Ware, *Orthodox Church*, 225, 261.

9. Parente, *Angels*, 112.

10. Colish, *Peter Lombard*; Lombard, *Works of Peter Lombard*, Vol. 2, bk. 2, ch. 1, 4–6.

11. Langton, *Supernatural*, 43–44, 52, 59.

12. Rorem, *Pseudo-Dionysius*, 77; Parente, *Angels*, 112.

consider the areas he wrote about. Just looking at the chapter headings in his *Summa Theologiae* tells all one needs to know about his approach:

- chapter 50. Of the Substance of the Angels Absolutely Considered

- chapter 51. Of the Angels in Comparison with Bodies

- chapter 52. Of the Angels in Relation to Place

- chapter 53. Of the Local Movement of the Angels

- chapter 54. Of the Knowledge of the Angels

- chapter 55. Of the Medium of the Angelic Knowledge

- chapter 56. Of the Angels' Knowledge of Immaterial Things

- chapter 57. Of the Angels' Knowledge of Material Things

- chapter 58. Of the Mode of the Angelic Knowledge

- chapter 59. The Will of the Angels

- chapter 60. Of the Love or Dilection of the Angels

- chapter 61. Of the Production of the Angels in the Order of Natural Being

- chapter 62. Of the Perfection of the Angels in the Order of Grace and of Glory

- chapter 107. The Speech of the Angels

- chapter 108. Of the Angelic Degrees of Hierarchies and Orders

- chapter 109. The Ordering of the Bad Angels

- chapter 110. How Angels Act on Bodies

- chapter 111. The Action of the Angels on Man

- chapter 112. The Mission of the Angels

- chapter 113. Of the Guardianship of the Good Angels

Of these twenty chapters specifically on angels (although they also crop up elsewhere, for example in discussion around demons), only two—the last two!—deal with what angels *do* here on earth. Aquinas, in the final analysis is not too focussed on looking at, practically, what angelic ministers *do*, and this theological tendency is still alive today, even outside Roman Catholic circles. Stephen Noll's book *Angels of Light, Powers of*

Darkness (1998) is classic example of this. It is without doubt a good book, one of the best in recent years. And yet, when one looks at his methodology, it is a direct throwback of nearly 1,000 years. In his section, *How to Approach Questions about Angels,* Noll says:[13] "Those who think seriously about angels find themselves asking two kinds of questions about them—ontological and epistemological . . . Ontological questions have to do with the nature of angels . . . Epistemological questions have to do with our knowledge of angels." Note that he adds no third category of what angels *do.* As with Aquinas, serious thinking about angels does not seem to include considering their *practical ministry to us.*

Roman Catholic Piety

How this incredible discussion and detail translated (or not) into medieval religious life has been the discussion of many academics. David Keck notes that while modern studies have ignored the practical and pastoral roles of angels, in the Middle Ages the people on the ground had not.[14] So, how would the average pious medieval Catholic have understood angels? The best examples are shown by the liturgies of the time, and here we see that angels, as intermediaries, were important. For example, one would pray: "Holy Michael, pray for us. Holy Gabriel, pray for us. Holy Raphael, pray for us. All ye holy Angels and Archangels of God, pray for us."[15] The *Mass of the Angels* has a prayer which asks: "Grant the perpetual help of thy mercy, O Lord, unto us, whom thou hast granted not to lack the ministrations of angels."[16]

One would also have specific masses for the three archangels (Michael, Gabriel, and Raphael), each one expounding in detail the benefits of their individual ministries. Raphael's would focus on healing, Michael's on protection, and Gabriel's had a broader focus: "O Gabriel, comfort the mourners, heal the sick, strengthen the weak, make us ever gentle and humble, and strong and established in the faith."[17]

There were also masses for specific circumstances in life. For example, the *Service for Pilgrims* invokes angelic protection for those

13. Noll, *Angels of Light, Powers of Darkness,* 27.

14. Keck, *Angels and Angelology,* 5.

15. Warren (trans.), *Sarum,* 1:277–80.

16. Ibid., 2:55–57.

17. Ibid., 2:224–26.

going on a journey: "May (God) send his angel Raphael to be your guardian in your pilgrimage; to conduct you on your way, in peace, to the place whither you would go, and to bring you back again in safety on your return to us."[18]

Angelic ministry is real and active on earth for the benefit of the people of God, and Roman Catholicism has to this day officially maintained this historic line. For example, the 1994 Catholic Catechism restated this position, basing it around Heb 1:14. Their presence stretches from Genesis to Revelation, and their ministry punctuates the whole of Christ's life. Angels have a real and practical, not theoretical nor symbolic, impact upon the church: "From infancy to death human life is surrounded by their watchful care and intercession. Beside each believer stands an angel as protector and shepherd leading him to life. Already here in earth the Christian life shares by faith in the blessed company of angels and men united in God."[19]

Recent Catholic theologians, such as Karl Rahner, have given little ground to modern influences (which we will discuss a little later), with more popular works by Daniélou, Parente, and Adler also holding the line.[20] However, one also saw thinkers such as Hans Küng, who while never denying angelic ministry, found little place for angels within voluminous and wide-ranging studies of church and theology.[21]

On a popular level, prior to the Reformation (and since), the ministry of angels was strong and vital, but, along with the saints, was almost replacing God as the focus of much popular piety, and this was reacted strongly against during the Reformation.

THE REFORMATION
(SIXTEENTH TO SEVENTEENTH CENTURIES)

Martin Luther (1483–1546)

It is interesting that Luther's disillusionment with the church began with the reissue of an Indulgence, which promised that angels would

---

18. Ibid., 2:170–73.

19. *Catholic Catechism*, 76–78, 599–601.

20. Rahner, *Encyclopaedia of Theology*, 6–13; Parente, *Angels*; Adler, *Angels and Us*; Daniélou, *Angels and their Mission*.

21. Küng, *The Church*; Küng, *On Being a Christian*; Küng, *Eternal Life*; Küng, *Does God Exist?*

remove souls from purgatory and ensure their safe journey to heaven.[22] Thus, Luther was bound to question how angels were viewed as he broke with Rome from 1518 onward. His attitude to scholastic angelology and Pseudo-Dionysius was harsh, calling his ideas *hallucinations*, and *laughable*, and the theology deserving to be *ridiculed*.[23] It was a *fanciful hodgepodge* that led men away from Christ.[24] However, despite this, angels are central to Luther's thought, and he started to recapture something of the pastoral and practical in angelology: "Let the beginning of all our affairs be prayer to God, and the next the thought of the care of angels."[25]

The existence and ministry of angels is an *ancient* and *heavenly* doctrine, known even by pagans, since in this life, empires, states, and households, and, in short, whatever this world has, are all governed by the ministry of holy angels.[26] God controls everything *through* his angels, who direct all human affairs, including the empires of the ungodly, intervening on God's behalf even in political decision-making. Angels have a twofold ministry—one to minister to creation, and one to worship God.[27] Everybody (Christian or not) has a guardian angel who influences their charge through reasoning with their mind, rather than as a supernatural altering of their thinking.[28] In the church men live *with the guardian angels*. In fact, where the church is, there is the ministry of angels.[29] Angels provide companionship, friendship and protection. They are peaceable, merciful, and kind, and they are there no matter how much people sin.[30] Angels protect houses, households and families, and people from demons.[31] As messengers, they guide and inspire people's thoughts *from without*, ceaselessly helping, counselling and pleading before God, in order to advance humankind, while God guides them *from within*.

---

22. Luther, *Luther's Works XXXVI*, 82, 148.
23. Ibid., XX:26; cf. XXIX, 121; XX, 64; XIII, 110–11.
24. Ibid., XXVI:109–10; LIV, 112; cf. Luther, *Table Talk*, VII.
25. Ibid., IV, 265.
26. Ibid., VI, 89–93; III, 62.
27. Ibid., VI, 92; cf. XXII, 201.
28. Ibid., IV, 265; cf. IV, 182, 256; XX, 170–72; cf. XX, 138.
29. Ibid., VIII, 60; XXII, 14, 20.
30. Ibid., IV, 255; cf. XX, 2, 179.
31. Ibid., III, 60; XXII, 208.

Nevertheless, Luther balanced this pastoral focus with criticism that rejected the place of angels as mediators and intercessors since there is not a single word of God's commanding us to call on either angels or saints, to intercede for us, and we have no examples of this in Scripture.[32] Angels cannot pay the ransom for sin, cannot sustain creation, cannot make one a son of God, and salvation does not depend on them. [33]

John Calvin and the Influence of Calvinism upon Angelology

John Calvin's (1509–1564) approach to angelology also exhibited a profound rejection of medieval angelology ("babblings of idle men"),[34] but it differed radically from Lutheranism. Echoing Augustine, Calvin refused to go beyond the explicitly Scriptural,[35] and was generally reluctant to find anything positive in the subject at all. He heavily restricted both the range and the study of angelology, arguably to the point that he, and his later followers, may as well have denied it.[36] Not only would anything not in Scripture not be examined, but only that which was *distinct and explicit* in Scripture would be considered. It is our (Christian) *duty* to remain in willing *ignorance* of angels, and one must direct one's mind to those things that are *edifying* and to *not indulge in curiosity, or studying things that are of no use.*

Calvin has done two things here. First, he warns the reader against investigation and speculation. Second, he asserts that angelology is not an edifying branch of theology and is of no use. Angelology is a hazardous subject, potentially misleading, and certainly superfluous.

Calvin's description of angelic ministry mirrors this and he says little beyond broad brush generalities.[37] Angels are ministers and dispensers of the divine bounty toward us who defend, guide, and watch for the elect's safety, and they take heed that no evil befall us.[38] However, nothing can be gained from knowing the mechanics of *how* this happens, and it would be wrong to assume that the only care God provides is the ministry of angels, as they are only one part of God's wider providence.

32. Ibid., XXXV, 198–99; cf. Luther, *Table Talk* CLXXVIII.

33. Ibid., XXII, 22, 27, 118, 346.

34. Calvin, *Institutes* I:XIV:4.

35. Schriener, *Theatre*, 39; cf. 52.

36. Ibid., 49.

37. Calvin, *Institutes* I:XIV:5; cf. I:XIV:9.

38. Ibid., I:XIV:6.

An understanding of angels is of no use in daily Christian life. Only a vague generalised recognition of angels in God's wider providence has any value to the average Christian man or woman. Luther's positive practicality has gone, and Calvin's method is to highlight Scriptural issues, and then pronounce the majority of them irrelevant or dangerous. Schriener sums it up well: "The limitation of angels (in Calvin's theology) was due to two factors. First, Calvin was attempting to abolish all idolatrous worship (and) the cult of angels . . . But Calvin's restriction of the power and authority of the angels is also indicative of his doctrine of providence as a whole, which never allowed real independence to secondary means."[39]

This last point highlights an important and enduring part of Calvin's approach. Calvin was in the middle of a fierce theological battle against Rome, and an important tactic was to undermine the whole basis of the Catholic sacramental system. One way to do this was to reject the idea of *secondary means*.[40]

Rome said that people gained grace and blessings unto salvation through involvement in the Mass, and via the whole sacramental system alongside the prayers of the saints and angels for you. In opposition, Calvin began with his doctrine of election where a person gained *everything* in terms of grace they need for full and perfect salvation in that single direct action of God. And if this were so, why would you need the extra sacramental grace, or the prayers of the saints, or ministry of angels? But Calvin didn't stop there. Not only does the full grace of election mean one essentially needs nothing else, even when God graciously does work upon a person, he works *directly*. He does not work through, for example, something else (something "secondary") like the Eucharist, baptism, or the oil of anointing, and their physical elements. If there are no secondary means, then God cannot and does not work through the sacramental system, so making the whole Roman scheme redundant.

As an apologetic tool this was highly effective, however, one cannot make arguments in isolation and they impact around themselves like a stone in a pool. As Scripture indicates, God sometimes uses angels instead of acting directly. Angels are God's *secondary means* par excellence. This presented a problem Calvin had to resolve. One cannot reject

---

39. Schriener, *Theatre*, 52–53.

40. This is a very much simplified version of a line of thought developed and demonstrated by my PhD.

secondary means, and keep angelic ministry in any meaningful sense. Calvin, to remain consistent to his wider thought and theology, had to reject *secondary means* as the normal way God works, and so sideline and limit angelic ministry. He confessed their existence, but focused their on-going role in heaven, while minimising any activity upon earth. He avoided saying guardian angels exist even though, as he admitted himself, there is good Scriptural and historical (Patristic) evidence for them.[41] Calvin knowing the weight of evidence, did not follow through and take a stance, but instead pleaded ignorance. Why? Admitting to the existence of guardian angels leads to the next question, "What do they do?" For their existence to be meaningful one would need to allow for secondary means as a part of how God works, and Calvin and his theology cannot allow this.[42] Calvin never excludes the technical possibility that God could work through secondary means (such as angels), since God, in his sovereignty can do as he pleases, but this theoretical possibility is never developed and remains just that, a theory.[43]

Angelic ministry becomes collateral damage, a theological sacrifice in order to win the greater battle. As a tactic for the period, one can understand it. However, it has never been properly corrected, and continues to be the glasses through which angels are viewed by many. Theodore Beza, Calvin's successor, refined Calvin's view, as did William Perkins, who in his *Golden Chain* (1595) limited the work of angels to heaven and made no attempt to extend their ministry earthward. Heaven and earth are effectively divorced as far as angelic ministry is concerned. He never denies the possibility, but equally writes not one word to say it could be.[44] The absence of teaching is as powerful and influential as any positive teaching. This approach continues to be taken as read by many, and a cessationist assumption (whether explicit or not) was engraved into Reformed theology. Many Reformed scholars confess the existence of angels but parallel it with no developed angelology and a refusal to see any ministry on earth, and so offer nothing more than modest summaries of biblical data before quickly passing onto other topics.[45] Beyond vague general providence, there is no meaningful angelic ministry

41. Calvin, *Institutes* I:XIV:7.

42. Macy, *Angels (1547–1662)*, ch. 5.

43. E.g., Calvin, *Institutes* I:14:11.

44. Brevard, *The Works of William Perkins: Golden Chain*, ch. 8.

45. Lane, *Unseen*, 10.

until Christ returns, and this remains the standard Reformed line to this day. So people such as Louis Berkof, Wolfhart Pannenberg, and Helmut Theilicke, while not wanting to deny the existence of angels, are overly cautious and avoid saying anything too concrete.[46]

Anglicanism

In direct contrast, and probably through the influence of Luther and a respect for the theological heritage of the church, the Church of England's liturgies kept angelic features and characteristics. Thomas Cranmer, in the *Book of Common Prayer*, over and against Calvinist influences, retained angels in both the liturgy and within the liturgical year, via the Feast of St Michael and all Angels (29th September). Cranmer rightly saw that a diminution of angelic ministry proposed by continental Calvinists did not do justice to the full witness of Scripture. Therefore, we read in the prayer for that day: "Everlasting God, which has ordained and consti- tuted the services of all Angels and men in a wonderful order: mercifully grant that they which always do Thee service in heaven, may by their appointment succour and defend us in earth: through Jesus Christ our Lord."[47] This is theologically rich, especially since it explicitly maintains the dual focus of service in heaven with ministry and work on earth, not divorcing two.

This relationship between angels and humans is further reinforced by the Sanctus which is prayed during the Eucharist. "Therefore *with Angels and Archangels, and with all the company of heaven*: we laude and magnify Thy glorious name, evermore, praising Thee, and saying: 'Holy, Holy, Holy, Lord God of Hosts, heaven and earth are full of your glory.'"

We, the congregation, pray *with* angels, *with* the company of heaven, and together *we* praise. This echoes the vision of Heb 12:22–23 of the joint society in the heavenly Jerusalem, and its reflection on earth in the church, where humans and angels make up the one united worshipping community. This communal aspect of *Book of Common Prayer* ensured a pastoral thread has been kept within the Anglican liturgy to this day, saying that angels and humanity were not discon- nected, but part of one united society which spanned heaven and earth.[48]

46. Berkof, *Systematic Theology*, 141–48; Pannenburg, *Systematic Theology (II)*, 102–9; Theilicke, *Evangelical Faith*, 363–64.

47. This prayer has remained in the Anglican liturgy since 1549.

48. Macy, *Pastoral Theology of the Angels*.

Richard Hooker (1554–1600), one of the greatest Anglican theologians, also resisted the Calvinist wish to divorce angels from the church, and he developed further Cranmer's thought, speaking beautifully of this one society: "For what is the assembling of the church to learn, but the receiving of angels descended from above. What to pray, but the sending of angels upwards."[49]

> The house of prayer [i.e., the church] is a court, beautified with the presence of celestial powers; *that there we stand, we pray, we sound forth hymns of praise to God, having his angels intermingled as our associates*; and that with reference hereunto, the apostle does require so great a care to be had of decency for the sake of angels; how can we come to the house of prayer, and not be moved by the very glory of the place itself, so to frame our affections praying, as does best beseem them, whose suits the Almighty does there sit to hear, and his angels attend to farther?[50]

Echoing the classic Jewish understanding, we go to church with the angels. They are *intermingled as our associates*. And just as our human brothers and sisters in Christ bless and uphold us pastorally, so too do the angels.

THE EARLY ENLIGHTENMENT
(SEVENTEENTH TO EIGHTEENTH CENTURIES)

However, the tide of history, thought, and philosophy began to flow against this, and Enlightenment thinking began to develop. Scientific exploration of the world, the planets, and the universe by people such as Gallileo, meant the more supernatural and miraculous aspects of Christianity were being questioned, then challenged, and finally rejected. The seventeenth century saw Descartes (1596–1650) sow the seeds of doubt—a doubt in everything. The only thing one could be sure of is that "I think, therefore I am." All else was uncertain, and while much uncertainty could be diffused by investigation (we know that animals exist because we can see and hold them), the angels, as spirit beings without physical bodies, were profoundly problematic.[51] Thomas Hobbes (1588–1679) mirrored this materialistic scepticism. ("Materialism,"

---

49. Hooker, *Of the Laws of Ecclesiastical Polity* V:23.

50. Ibid., 25:2, quoting Chrysostom, *Hom. Heb.* 15; cf. Chrysostom, *Hom. Act.* 24.

51. Descartes, *Meditations* (2) 24–25; (3) 43.

in this context, means believing only in that which could be held and examined.) Reacting against scholastic theology, he created an early form of demythologization, where he said that the vast majority of angelic stories in Scripture could be explained without resorting to saying that immaterial spirit beings existed.[52] Hobbes, as a materialist, believed that only beings with physical bodies could exist, so "spirit being" was a literal contradiction in terms. Therefore, God supplied visions or direct encounters, which people called "angels." God did not do it through intermediary spirit beings, since *spirit* equals non-being, and thus non-existence. Even though Bishop John Bramhall successfully challenged this assertion (since, if beings of spirit cannot exist, then God cannot exist),[53] the basic problem of the non-investigability of angels as spirit beings has continued.

John Locke (1632–1704) further developed this materialist line by denying the possibility of the human mind to apprehend anything beyond that which our five senses and intuition can take in. However, Locke does not fully follow through on his position, saying that it is possible for other worlds or beings to exist, which we know nothing of. But that is the point. We know nothing of them, and can know nothing of them. He recognises that Scripture says angels do exist, and can't find any reasons to conclusively say they do not, yet has nothing to say they do either.[54]

Investigability, and the openness to experimental demonstration was, and still is, a dominant theme in the Post-Enlightenment scientific method. If one cannot rationally observe, examine, and scrutinise something, or at least its effects, then one must doubt its reality. Angels and the unseen created realm were, and continue to be, problematic.

THE EIGHTEENTH AND NINETEENTH CENTURIES

I mentioned earlier how God had become increasingly distant for a variety of reasons. This found a renewed focus in the rise of deism, a rationalistic understanding of religion which said that God created the world and then departed, leaving humans to it. God was revealed in two

52. It is of note that in *Leviathan* (Sec. 209–14) Hobbes, after a long discussion saying that angels do not exist, eventually says they do, solely on of the words of Christ, and not due to any problem with his methodology.

53. Bramhall, *Works of John Bramhall*, Vol. IV, 535–36.

54. Locke, *An Essay on Human Understanding*, 4:11:12; cf. 3:6:12.

ways—the visible creation, and an inner moral law by which humans could know right and wrong. Deism rejected that God had revealed himself through prophets, visions, angels, miracles, or any inspired writings. It rejected the explicitly supernatural in favour of pragmatic moralism, and so it is of no surprise that angels played no part in this theological and philosophical movement. Deism became popular all over Enlightenment Europe, and held sway in many pulpits. However deism was skilfully combated by Joseph Butler and his *Analogy Of Religion* (1736). Deism's focus on reason over revelation, led Butler to say that revealed truth was supplemental to the religious knowledge that could be gained from the examination of nature. Revelation should not overrule reason, so if any biblical teaching appeared to be immoral or in contradiction to the knowledge acquired by man's natural faculties, it was necessary to seek another interpretation of that Scripture. This view of faith and revelation meant that Butler was little interested in the more spiritual or metaphysical matters. While his book deftly defeated deism, it did so at the cost of having virtually no understanding of angels within it. Butler does speak of an invisible world, and invisible influences and forces, but never angels, and so indicates that there is an angelic *realm*, but it is pointedly undeveloped and when it is mentioned never dwelt upon.[55]

However, not all eighteenth century theologians followed this line. John Wesley (1703–1791) had a strong understanding of and belief in angels. In his sermon *Of Good Angels* (based around Heb 1:14) he explains that the nature and origin of angels can only be known by revelation, and beyond the bounds of human investigation by their very nature. Angels, holy, wise, and strong—beyond our comprehending—can see into the human heart and minister to humans in a deep way:

> They may assist us in our search after truth, remove many doubts and difficulties, throw light on what was before dark and obscure, and confirm us in the truth that is after godliness. They may warn us of evil in disguise; and place what is good, in a clear, strong light. They may gently move our will to embrace what is good, and fly from that which is evil. They may, many times, quicken our dull affections, increase our holy hope or filial fear, and assist us more ardently to love Him who has first loved us.[56]

55. Butler, *The Analogy Of Religion* I:1:3; I:3:4; I:4; I:5:4; I:7:1, 2; I:Conclusion; 2:1:2; 2:2:1; 2:4:1; 2:51.

56. Wesley, *Of Good Angels,* 2:2.

With Wesley, we have an indication that interest in the true pastoral ministry of angels had neither ceased, nor been totally forgotten. However, time marched onward, and a dynamic understanding of angels and their ministry became increasingly sidelined and minimised. Friedrich Schleiemacher (1768–1834) further strengthened the foundations of an angel-less universe, but did so on the basis on an understanding of a God who can be experienced directly.[57] He never denied the theoretical possibility of angels, but made the criteria for accepting their existence so strict it was never realistically an option.[58] Schleiermacher, however, saw the value of angels in a liturgical sense, and so along with many in the Victorian romantic milieu, held the double value of rejecting their existence, while promoting them as a romantic, mythical, and sentimental concept which may help or inspire one's spirituality. [59]

But in addition to the ability to hold the seemingly inconsistent belief that non-existent beings are helpful to one's spirituality, Schleiermacher strongly made the case that, even though Christ, the apostles, and the New Testament writers spoke clearly and unambiguously about angels and their ministry, it by no means indicates that they actually believed in them. He made the point that people speak of fairies, ghosts, and other fanciful things, without actually believing in them. Therefore, one was now able to circumvent the plain words of the Bible, since one did not have to take literally what Christ or the apostles said, since they need not have meant what they said.[60]

After Schleiermacher, biblical criticism gained pace. F. D Strauss (1808–1874) reinforced this deep scepticism in his highly influential *Life of Jesus* (1835/1836), with which many in the modern critical tradition would still broadly agree: "(Events) which were formerly thought to be wrought by God himself through the ministering angels, we now are able to explain by natural causes; so that belief in angels is without a link by which it can attach itself to rightly apprehended modern ideas; and it exists only as a lifeless tradition . . . If it be true that God is immanent in the world, precisely on that account is the intervention of angels rendered superfluous."[61] Angels and their ministry are a lifeless

57. Schleiermacher, *Faith*, Sec. 4, 34–35.

58. Ibid., 42:1; 16:3; 17:2.

59. Ibid., 42:2.

60. Ibid., 42:2.

61. Strauss, *Life of Jesus*, vol. I, 82–83.

tradition, superfluous to God's direct action up the earth. This attitude has pervaded much of the theology since Strauss, only being refined further, as opposed to challenged or questioned. Angels are not only illogical and superfluous, they are now also irrelevant.

TWENTIETH CENTURY THEOLOGICAL INFLUENCES

Bultmann and Barth

Modern scholarship, looking back to Strauss and Schleiermacher, has strongly questioned traditional biblical cosmology and its understanding of angels. Rudolph Bultmann (d. 1974) was clear that angels do not exist, and taking Schleiermacher's thought to the extreme, "angel" is simply is mythological or linguistic tool to aid an understanding of God. And however some may nuance it, there is a significant strand of modern theology which does not believe in angels, and would concur with Bultmann's claim that, "It is impossible to use electric light and the wireless and to avail ourselves of modern medical and surgical discoveries, and at the same time believe in the New Testament world of spirits and miracles."[62]

Generally there has been a move within theology, reflected by writers such as John McQuarrie, to follow Bultmann.[63] Others see the angelic (especially demons) as a literary tool to explain how the inexplicable could happen in a universe created and ruled by God.[64] Some, like Tillich ("if they exist")[65] find their presence in texts too difficult to decipher and demythologise. Therefore, a theological tradition has grown which finds angels of questionable practical and theological value, with issues of hermeneutics and methodology impossible to unravel to any satisfactory level.

Reacting against Bultmannesque demythologisation, however, we have Karl Barth (d. 1969).[66] Osborn summarises Barth's attitude: "Angels are a scandal to the rational mind, summoning us to take seriously the task of *faith seeking understanding* that is, listening to the

---

62. Bultmann, *New Testament and Mythology* in Bartsch, ed., *Kerygma and Myth* I, 5.

63. McQuarrie, *Principles*, 233–37.

64. Pagels, *Origin of Satan*, xvi.

65. Tillich, *Systematic Theology*, 260.

66. Barth, *Church Dogmatics*, 3:3369ff.

primary witness of Scripture."[67] Angels are "ministering spirits," who can only be known through God's revelation. Since the term "spirits" is one we cannot truly understand, we can only consider angels through their "ministering." Therefore Barth's angelology is function-focussed. Angels witness to and accompany God's actions on earth, which means that God acts directly, and angels seem to be little more than signposts which point to where God has acted. They themselves seem to do little, which again highlights the on-going struggle with the question of secondary means. Nevertheless, it is their nature and existence to serve God, and be at his disposal to serve humankind. Angels are citizens of heaven, the mystery of creation, and both bear and herald that mystery to humanity, and this is crucial: "A world without angels would be a world without wonder. A theology without angels is a theology without mystery, and if our theology cannot accommodate the mystery of creation (heaven), in the end it will fail to accommodate God."[68] Barth is here mirroring Bishop Bramhall's comments 300 years earlier, that if you struggle with the concept of spirit and spirit beings, you will eventually struggle with the basic idea of God.

Barth confesses the existence of angels, as he must, but effectively limits their ministry to peripheral roles.[69] Nevertheless, Barth warns against *the angelology of the shrug of the shoulders*,[70] where the supernatural realm of heaven is removed as a focal point of Christianity and earthly, moral, practical concerns are focused upon to the exclusion of the heavenly. An angelology which doesn't really engage with the subject, Barth contends, is at best *impossible* or at least *profoundly unsatisfactory*.[71] It is *credo ut intelligam*—one cannot affirm that Scripture speaks of angels and then happily move onward ignorant of what this means. And yet, despite this, Barth ultimately struggles to make angels truly applicable to the Christian life.

(It is worth noting that there have also been some recent books which have tried to defend the existence of angels from the stand point of apologetics. Two of the best are *The Angels and Us* by Mortimer Alder, and *The Case for Angels* by Peter Williams. Both of these books

67. Lane, *Unseen*, 21.

68. Lane, *Unseen*, 35.

69. Ibid., 37.

70. Barth, *Church Dogmatics* 3:3, 413.

71. Ibid., 3:3, 418.

argue—through the use of philosophy, mathematics, and physics—that the existence of an unseen angelic realm is rational possibility worthy of proper consideration and not to be simply ridiculed. While not pastoral in focus, they nonetheless realize that angels are not a throw-away part of Christian faith and religion, and are important for properly understanding our universe.)

Walter Wink

Walter Wink, Professor Emeritus of Biblical Interpretation at Auburn Theological Seminary, wrote a number of influential books, in the 1980s and 1990s, which attempted to recover and re-evaluate the biblical descriptions of angelic and demonic powers.

Wink's central theme is that heavenly powers exist, and have a tangible impact on peoples' lives. However, the distinctive move that Wink makes is that he does not see angels or demons as single personal entities, since it *is merely a habit of thought that makes people think of the Powers as personal beings.*[72] For Wink, the "Powers" are the actual spirituality of systems and structures that have either betrayed (demons) or accepted (angels) their divine vocation.[73] However, despite clear belief in the immanent reality of angelic powers as *intermediary realities in a fallen world,*[74] Wink gives short shrift to guardian angels and similar individualised and personalised understandings of angels as *disembodied spirits in the air.*[75] In fact, Wink tends to lump all angelic activity in under the category of "powers," and fails to take seriously the wide range of biblical designations, many of which are individualised and also transcendent.[76] So while Wink's vision is fascinating and influential, one struggles to see how it describes the full biblical revelation and description of angels in all their forms and roles.

Graham, Grudem, and Goll

Billy Graham wrote the hugely successful *Angels: God's Secret Agents* (1975) because little had been written on them that century within

72. Wink, *Engaging*, 8.

73. Ibid., 8–9; cf. 309–10.

74. Lane, *Unseen*, 25.

75. Wink, *Powers that Be*, 23–24.

76. Lane, *Unseen*, 25–26.

his evangelical Protestant context. This seemed a strange and ominous omission.[77] His book contains no great revelations, nor new theological insights into the area, and Graham is careful not to go beyond the biblical evidence, but nonetheless tackles some of the more speculative areas of angelology. Initial chapters, while having quite snappy titles, plainly use the scholastic categories. Angels are not abstract theological concepts, but truly ministering spirits sent by God, and so Graham moves through the book looking to more practical issues, including one chapter on *Angels in Our Lives Today*. Here Graham relates stories of angelic encounters and ministry, seeing angels active in present day life (and death). However while it might be described as written from a pastoral and practical standpoint, it struggles to really integrate the stories with the theology. It was an important book, rightly refocusing people on the reality of angels, but it never truly got to the heart of the matter.

Similarly influential has been Wayne Grudem's *Systematic Theology*.[78] Nothing of Grudem's work is ground-breaking, yet that such an influential evangelical author posits such a clearly positive angelology is important. It is also interesting that he aims to apply his theology at a practical and pastoral level, and engages with the more speculative areas of angelology finding practical applications. In good scholastic fashion, Grudem begins by considering the angelic nature and creation, mentioning that guardian angels are unlikely, but nevertheless that angelic protection is real. Angels show the greatness of God's love and plan for humans, and remind us that the unseen world is real. Angels are exemplars, in both their obedience and worship, *and provide helpful examples for us to imitate*. Angels carry out some of God's plans and will, bring messages to humans, and directly glorify God. Grudem also discusses the relationship between humans and angels, stating that we worship with the angels, angels see our disobedience and are grieved by it, and that their witness and occasional visits should keep Christians alert to how they live their lives. Humans should be prepared to attribute amazing events to their intervention, and thank God for their ministry, visible and invisible. In Grudem one starts to see that maybe a richer route is available to understanding angels, and a pastoral application is truly possible, yet he himself is highly cautious about expecting too much from angels today.

77. Graham, *Angels*, ix.

78. Grudem, *Systematic Theology*, 397–411.

Other charismatic writers are more open to looking at the applied or practical, but seemingly always at a cost. For example, James Goll in his *Angelic Encounters*[79] relates how angels are ministering in powerful and amazing ways today. However, his grasp of the fullness of the theology surrounding angels is poor, and while much of what he says is clearly mirrored by Scripture, other things seem to slip through the net of examination. There is a lack of real integration of theology and experience, and systematic working through of the two areas.

New Age Spirituality

As a challenge to many Christians, Laurence Osborn makes an insightful point about modern spirituality in a postmodern world. He says the rejection of the angelic is implicitly deist and denies the spiritual and supernatural which many seek. By not speaking about the angelic the church is missing a large group of people, especially, but not only, those influenced by the wide range of New-Age spiritualities: "New-agers do not regard angels as the stuff of speculation. On the contrary, their fascination with angels is driven by a very practical desire for a wholeness that integrates physical, psychological, and spiritual realities. That fascination and desire are potentially important bridge points."[80] Any quick book search on Amazon will reveal what a huge market and interest is out there. In direct contrast to the cautious, ambivalent, or theologically weak writings about angels by many Protestant Christians, Spiritualists and New-Agers have taken them to their hearts.

Doreen Virtue is one of many writers in this vein. Going to the opposite extreme, she has produced an almost purely pastoral, and totally applied, vision of angels—an understanding which is deeply personalised and tangible. However, she does so by shedding virtually every possible theological anchor. While she claims to be Christian, it is not the Christianity that would be recognised by any orthodox or historic branch of the faith. Her dynamic understanding of the ministry of angels is underpinned by a thinly veiled syncretism, probable unitarianism, definite pantheism, a belief in reincarnation, and an assumed universalism. She seems unclear quite who/what God is; calling God mother and father

79. Goll & Goll, *Angelic Encounters*.
80. Lane, *Unseen*, 46.

in one place, but a force in another.[81] Whoever God is, she/he/it needs the personal touch of the angelic to function, which feels like a throwback to the assumptions which drove Pseudo Dionysius. God is not particularly personal, nor close, but angels are. When one reads Virtue's books it is surprising (or not!) how little God is actually mentioned, and when God is talked of, there is little detail or focus. In this light it is not surprising that angels, not God particularly, give a huge range of answers to various questions. For example: [82]

- How can I discover what my life purpose is?
- How can I feel happier?
- Why do my prayers go unanswered?
- Dolphins seem to be unearthly, and I wonder what their origin is and if they have a special purpose on the earth.
- How can I know that my current love partner is my soul mate?
- I am thinking about going into business for myself, but I'm not sure if it is the right thing to do. How can I know if self-employment is the right thing for me or not?

This list, if nothing else, is both conversational and pastorally focussed, speaking directly to people. Virtue has plainly tapped into a need in people, recognising that people yearn for spirituality, and can empathise with the idea of angelic ministry in a personal and direct way. Yet she has done so without any theological grounding or recognisably orthodox Christian anchor. This has led to a presentation of angels that, while it has some external parallels to the biblical view of the angelic, scratching beneath the surface shows that it has departed a long way from Scripture. It borrows indiscriminately from many sources, and is more than a little indebted to various westernised versions of eastern philosophies.

CONCLUSION

This whistle-stop tour of church history highlights a few things. It is true that while the pastoral angle of the ministry of angels is rarely totally ignored, it is increasingly sidelined, with an ever-decreasing interest in true application. Discussions grow more distant and disconnected, and

81. Virtue, *Messages*, 122.
82. Ibid., 91–118.

presentations become mainly theory with only a smattering of pastoral application, at best. Those writers who do develop the pastoral aspects more often than not do so with highly variable, at times rather dubious, theological rooting and outcomes. The recent resurgence of interest in angels has either been too rooted in previous ways, or it has been so freed from the past that it is unrooted and baseless in any recognisable Christian theology. Neither way is satisfactory.

In contrast, the prominent biblical presentation of angels is pastoral, practical, and applied. Therefore, we need to invert the prevailing methods, while not loosing them from Scripture. The Enlightenment idea that one should not expect angels to show up for dinner clashes directly with the biblical exhortation to be prepared *exactly* for that event, and more. Angels, sent and commissioned by God, do intervene in our lives, but how does this happen and how are we are to understand it? It is to these questions we now turn.

3

Why a Pastoral Theology of the Angels?

IS THERE A BETTER WAY?

THE WAY THAT ANGELS have traditionally been considered hasn't helped us get a balanced or proper understanding of them or what they do. None of the approaches seen in the previous chapter are satisfying because none do justice to how the Bible presents angels. The Bible, instead of wallowing in speculative wonderings, gives us a sober and practical picture of who angels are and what they *do*. This suggests that to view angels rightly, one needs practical and pastoral lenses in our theological glasses. However, the idea of a pastoral theology of angels looks strange, because pastoral theology is conceived in terms in which angels do not fit neatly, but when one steps back, this way of looking at angels makes much more sense of what we see in the Bible.

The aim of pastoral theology is to focus people back to God when they have lost their way, and bring them back into a godly wholeness of life. Pastoral angelology is no different. Just as your vicar or pastor is serving God, and helping you live a better and fuller Christian life, so angels are God's angels, and not autonomous beings who act independently of the Triune Godhead. Just like your minister, all pastoral and ministerial functions of angels should begin with, and return to, God (for his glory and will), with the aim of leading you closer to Jesus.

Clearly the category of *pastoral angelology*, like most theological categories, is not plainly and neatly expounded in the Bible, and so some thinking around verses and passages (especially in the light of traditional readings) is needed. As the last chapter showed us, many historic attempts at understanding angels have been prone to assumption and large leaps of logic, which have been rightly criticised, in, for example, the numerous biting attacks of Reformation and later Enlightenment.

We all know the story of the theologians who debated how many angels could dance on the head of a pin—a classic example of a futile argument. This debate was pointless, so surely the whole subject is pointless. While I honor the wish of others to challenge poor theology, I note that these criticisms not only ignore the fact that behind the debates was an honest desire to understand how the spiritual and physical worlds inter-relate, but the critics usually had nothing to replace what they shot down, and they themselves ended up in an impoverished dead end.

Let's look at the biblical texts for what they say, with as few preconceived ideas as possible.

PASTORAL THEOLOGY

What is pastoral theology? *A Dictionary of Pastoral Care* gives us a nice simple description.[1] It begins with the idea that one presents a vision of God in order to show:

- Love, care, and concern for the individual.

- Responsibility for groups in society.

- Spiritual direction.

Just from this initial description, you can see how angels can play a part in all of these areas. One can also see that the three broad categories used bear little relation to the models and frameworks described in the last chapter. They are not scholastically influenced categories that invite speculative investigation, but ones that look for a consistently practical application. These categories can be further defined, but how this is done depends on the specific pastoral theology model you use. Of the many possible models, I will use one described in Clebsch & Jaekle's *Pastoral Care in Historical Perspective*,[2] because it is a simple, classic, and foundational model,[3] which is easily applicable. Clebsch & Jaekle define pastoral care as "consisting of helping acts, done by representative Christian persons, directed toward the healing, sustaining, guiding, and reconciling of troubled persons whose troubles arise in the context of ultimate meanings and concerns."[4] Of course, this definition presupposes that the ministers in view are human; but need we make such an as-

1. Campbell, *Pastoral Care*, 188–90, 192–93.

2. Clebsch and Jaekle, *Pastoral*.

3. Lartey, *In Living Color*, 21.

4. Clebsch and Jaekle, *Pastoral*, 4.

sumption? Don't angels also do helping acts, as representatives of God? Don't they also meet troubled people? Don't they, by their angelic presence, give someone a wider context to consider, a context which lifts the person out of earthly present and into the very throne room of God? The answer to these questions must be "Yes." Yet do angels enact a pastoral role which can be investigated as a pastoral theology? Clebsch & Jaekle's give four furthers areas to consider, which define closely whether something counts as pastoral theology or not:[5]

1. Healing—promoting physical and spiritual wholeness.

2. Sustaining—building a faith that can grow and last.

3. Guiding—recognising and making (moral) decisions.

4. Reconciling—both God and neighbour.

These four areas must be present for a theology to be truly counted as pastoral, since together they provide the holistic approach needed.

(1) Healing

The question of what healing is, is common within churches. It is recognised that healing is a multifaceted thing, which touches people on many levels. Healing (of body, mind, or spirit) is not just restoration, but also aims to lift one up, so that that *the troubled person will become integrated on a higher spiritual level than he had previously experienced.*[6] Healing takes one to a new place, with a tangible change occurring in that journey.

Healing can come in many forms. At one extreme, it may be the miraculous divine intervention which confounds medical science, leading one to open (or reopen) one's spiritual eyes to a God who is alive and active in the here and now. At the other end of the spectrum it might be the circumstance where, for example, one is gravely ill, and forced to look at life afresh. Illness can cause us to reconsider life and wonder about our priorities. What was once important now seems irrelevant. Worrying about money, status, and petty grudges with loved ones suddenly seems so silly. And those things in life once deemed of little importance, such as prayer and praise to God, and quality time for both blood and church

---

5. Ibid., 32–66.

6. Ibid., 33.

family, now strike home as the central planks of a rounded and healthy life. Illness, or any life shaking event, focuses us on personal mortality and frailty. And when we consider these things, our eyes are turned toward the God of life, the God of both the now and the hereafter. This re-evaluation of life, and the re-ordering of priorities and worldview, speaks of a healing of mind and spirit, away from worldly attitudes and toward more Godly perspectives. This reflection awakens people to (re) dedicate themselves to God, thus bringing renewal to the soul.

(2) Sustaining

The journey of life is long, and has many hills, bumps, corners and pot-holes to negotiate. You need to be sustained on this voyage. It is natural then that God gives us sustenance through life, and does so in many ways through the ministry of the church. Clebsch & Jaekle say that the ministry of sustaining has four aspects to it.

First, pastoral care *preserves* the situation with as little loss as pos-sible. When one is in a hole, one always fears that the bottom will never come, and there is always further to fall. Preservation aims to stop you falling further, and to hold the line against other threats, further loss, or excessive retreat.[7] Second, building on preservation, is the *consolation* that the problem does not negate one's destiny in God, and that you are not alone in your distress. In the midst of suffering comes relief from misery and acknowledgment of the damaging and robbing experience. There might not be a solution as such, but you get the shoulder to cry on, the comforting hug, or the encouraging word to keep you going.[8]

Yet keeping going is difficult when you feel shaky and uncertain, so you need to *consolidate* what you have to build a platform from which to then face life. Even when you stop falling, you think that you don't have what it takes to get out of the hole. With the misery soothed, resources can be marshalled to face the future. Hope is built by seeing that any loss is a partial loss, not a total loss. Hope remains and can be built upon.[9] Consolidation is the renewal of a right perspective on life, and with this foundation laid, a new start can begin—which Clebsch and Jaekle call "redemption." Obviously this *redemption* is not that which Christ gives.

---

7. Ibid., 44.

8. Ibid., 47.

9. Ibid., 47.

It is not salvation. Redemption is the new start found by facing, then embracing the loss. The loss is not necessarily restored, since this would be healing, but it is starting the journey, to *begin* to build an ongoing life that once more pursues its fulfilment and destiny on a new basis. [10]

(3) *Guiding*

Now you have started the next leg of your journey, which direction do you choose? You do not want to walk into another problem or hole, but you want the paths that God wants for you. You want guidance. Guidance has four aspects which define it.

First is *advice-giving*, which includes discipline. It is words given when the thing you most need is true knowledge and insight given by a wise counsellor. It is also the wisdom which seeks to bring a person into a situation which will be conducive to their welfare, especially when it entails leading them out of a negative situation. The first type of wisdom assumes a place to build from exists and can be used. The second type guides one to a place, from which one can then build. It is a wisdom that recognises whether you are standing on the edge of the cliff ready to jump, or have already moved away from the edge and are looking for what to do next. A good example of this is evangelism, since a relationship with Christ is always the best starting point for anybody. However, it can also be the simple word which puts you on the right path into the wisdom or the help you need, which may, many years down the line, have been the seed which was sown and now sprouts unto salvation.[11]

The second is called *devil-craft*, which is the ability to stand against Satan. On your journey you will be opposed, and Satan can do this in many ways. Guidance in *devil-craft* helps you avoid these pit-falls. First, is not be isolated, but to be joined—interlocked in faith—with other believers. Together in the church and under the word (following Scripture), one can resist Satan and his schemes. Isolation is a key tactic of Satan and his cohorts, and one needs to be guided back to Christ's body for sustenance and protection.[12] *Devil-craft* can also include exorcism and removal of demonic oppression, where the hindering of one's

---

10. Ibid., 48.
11. Ibid., 50–51.
12. Ibid., 51–52.

walk with God is more clearly seen and experienced, and thus more easily removed.

The third part of guidance is, strangely, silence. It is *listening*. You are not able to guide properly unless you know what the problem truly is. And to find that out, you need to stop and listen. Clarifying a situation needs you to listen to the problem being spoken out. Listening can allow a troubled person to unburden themselves, and verbalise the sadness, frustration and anger that may be felt. Allowing people to let off steam in a safe context can be very helpful. Listening can also help you accurately reflect back what was being said, and allow the person to hear and gain understanding of how they feel.[13] Listening lets you to be a mirror for the person to look into, and be challenged by their own words. This is a very powerful skill in pastoral care.

And finally, advice-giving is simple help in decision making, to encourage and promote wise and helpful conclusions and courses of action.[14]

(4) *Reconciling*

Now on the journey, and heading in the right direction, one never wants to journey alone, nor travel with people with whom you are in conflict. We all want our journey through life to be as peaceful as possible. Therefore, the fourth area Clebsch and Jaekle speak of is the ministry of reconciliation. Distinct from, and not to be confused with, the ultimate act of reconciliation through God in Christ, this aims to bring people into a position to be reconciled to both God, and others around them. It is the healing of broken relationships. This can takes two basic forms. First is forgiveness *which can be a proclamation, or an announcement, or even a very simple gesture indicating that,* in spite of walls of pride and hurt which separate and alienate people, *something has occurred to re-establish and reunite persons to each other, and, indeed, to God.*[15] How many times have our lives been hampered by us holding grudges which would much better be soothed with the balm of forgiveness and the gift of a restored friendship? How many times has this broken relationship

---

13. Ibid., 53–54.
14. Ibid., 54.
15. Ibid., 57.

been with our brothers and sisters, as well as with God? Forgiveness restores and heals.

Second is discipline, which includes friendly words of correction, "priestly" admonishments, or even sterner measures directed toward confession, repentance, and amendment of life.[16] Discipline keeps us on the right path, and can either protect or restrain, or even provoke a reaction to make one think seriously about a situation. But however the discipline comes, it aims to keep the Christian within the church and within healthy, godly relationships, protected from temptation and assault.

One Plank of Many

This is a rich understanding of pastoral theology. However, one can imagine that for it to work, a vicar or pastor needs a range of tools. It can be done through Sunday worship and sermons, through one-to-one meetings, through midweek groups, and through prayer groups. One method alone will not make this model work. Similarly, it must be recognized that pastoral angelology cannot be taken as a stand-alone approach, but must be part of a wider integrated theology and practice. If a church does not have a developed understanding of pastoral theology and practice, and/or the supernatural intervention of God to meet people in their need, then this will be of little use. Unconnected and unrelated to a wider vision of God and his ministry, pastoral angelology will struggle to have any effect. Also, if this is applied to the exclusion of other pastoral care, it will also fail. As Ps 91 says, angels are one part of a wider will and system, and must not be detached from that. Therefore, as another plank within an already existing pastoral vision, angels have a positive and inspiring place, making Heb 1:14 a day-to-day reality.

HOW DO ANGELS MINISTER?

Now we have laid the basic foundations for a pastoral theology, we need to consider "how" angels minister. Clebsch and Jaekle's book has many examples of how human ministers implement pastoral care, but what about angels? How do angels bring this pastoral ministry to us? The Bible suggests that angels help us in three ways:

---

16. Ibid.

1. Angels can demonstrate to us (as an exemplar or role-model), or tell us, how we may live.

2. Angels can walk or stand alongside us, acting as an encouraging or battling companion.

3. Angels can work upon, or within, us.

Demonstrating, Telling, or Promoting to Us, What We Should Do and How We Should Be

The role of angels as *messengers* is perhaps the most obvious and well known. They come with words of encouragement, warning, and guidance, and these are given through physical appearances, appearances in visions and dreams, or by them speaking from heaven.[17] The angels direct what the person to whom they appear should do, and so shape their subsequent actions for the better. Angels can also influence in other ways. For example, we humans are on a stage before them that requires us to be aware of how we live and act, and St Paul also demands proper order in church "because of the angels" (1 Cor 11:10). Similarly, the principle of rebuking sinners so that others will be watchful of their own lives is underpinned by knowing one is before the angels: "I solemnly charge you in the presence of God and of Christ Jesus and his chosen angels, to maintain these principles without bias, doing nothing in a spirit of partiality." (1 Tim 5:21). We are in front of angels, and their presence alongside Christ (the Son) and God (the Father) means we need to seriously consider how we live our lives.

Coming to, Walking with, or Standing alongside Us

The idea of the journeying angel has a long and rich tradition. It is classically shown in the Apocryphal book of Tobit, where the Archangel Raphael guides Tobit through numerous trials and tribulations to ultimate success for the glory of God. This is not unique to the Apocrypha. Hagar, who had run away from Abraham and Sarah, was met on her journey by an angel sent by God, who encouraged her to return (Gen 16:7–12). Similarly, God promised an angel would go before the Israelites to lead them into the Promised Land, and defeat their enemies in front of them (Exod 33:2). 2 Kgs 6:17 is an amazing example of angels

---

17. E.g., Gen 16:7–12; 21:17; Luke 1:26–38; John 12:28–29; Acts 27:23–24.

standing alongside God's people in times of need and distress. The King of Syria's army was surrounding the city, and Elisha's servant, naturally, was badly panicked by this. However, Elisha was at peace because he saw God's angelic army was there too, and could defeat the Syrians. The servant needed his eyes opened by God to this truth (as a lesson to us all), and only then did he know the scale of God's angelic protection in the time of need. One last example would be Elijah, in the desert, starving and desperate, who had an angel meet him, to give him food and water and encourage him on his journey to God's mountain—where God would meet him (1 Kgs 19:4–8).

Working on or within Us

This is possibly the most difficult of the three areas, especially since, on some levels, it will look similar to how the Holy Spirit may act. However, surface comparisons are soon dissipated when looked at more carefully, and it will be shown that while angels can influence us in that manner, it is in no way synonymous to the depth or quality or profundity of the work of the Spirit within. The Spirit is the one who regenerates, the one who actually works the inner-transformation, the one who changes and makes us sons and daughters of God. Angels cannot do this—this is solely a work of God. But angels can prompt and stir us in our hearts and minds in a way similar to how the Spirit may do so.

Generally, angels are able to speak to us via non-physical means, for example, through dreams, as Joseph experienced (Matt 1:20–21). Angels are also able to entice people, as the story of the angelic spirit in 1 Kgs 22:19–23 demonstrates. God asks which of the angelic spirits would entice King Ahab, enticement being a form of persuasion. The angelic spirit achieved this end by giving the prophets, unbeknown to them, certain words to speak. The spirit enticed one, by directing the words of others. Angels can, quite simply, get in our heads and speak to us, to influence us and our actions, without us necessarily knowing it. Yet this is a little vague and to know what it may mean to be guided by an angel, more detail is needed.

ANGELIC INFLUENCE (LUKE 8:26–39)

This key question over how much angels can influence what we do and think is not clearly addressed in Scripture, yet has been much discussed over the centuries. However, while the Bible tells us little about what the good angels can do, it does say what fallen angels are capable of. Therefore one can infer that if demons can negatively influence in certain ways, then holy angels can, under God's direction, motivate in positive ways. Luke 8:26–39 and the man possessed by "Legion" highlights this most clearly (cf. Mark 5:1–20), and it gives us various principles from which we can work.

1. Many angels can influence one human at the same time—Legion was "many" (Luke 8:30)

2. This influence can shape one's life and reaction to circumstances around oneself, and can do so on an ongoing basis. The possessed man would not wear clothes, he would not live with people, he spent his time around corpses, and he would run into the mountains and solitary places (Luke 8:27–29; cf. Mark 5:5). The demons had successfully isolated him ("devil-craft").

3. The angelic influence can give or promote strength and ability beyond normal human behaviour. The man could break chains and escape from human bonds (Luke 8:29).

4. This influence, however, did not totally override the human will. It is worth noting that while the demons in the man wanted to escape from Jesus, the man actually ran *toward* Jesus and *fell before* him, and the man *remained* there (Luke 8:27–28; cf. Mark 5:6). The possessed man saw Jesus from a distance. If the demons wanted to escape they could have simply run in the opposite direction, but the man did not. The man's will to meet Jesus overrode the demons' wish not to meet Jesus. However, the man's will could not then speak to Jesus as he wanted to, because he was under the influence of the demons. The demons spoke, but could not drive the man away from Christ. The man remained at his feet, in opposition to what the demons spoke and wanted.

This suggests that while angelic influence can be very strong, it is never total. It will never keep one away, or obscure one, from meeting Jesus if that is what the person truly wills. Similarly, the demons could not kill the man, even though it was their destructive intent to do so—look at what happened to the pigs, which could not resist the demons. Their first action was to kill themselves. The man had lived, miserably to be sure, yet he lived. The (demonic) angelic influence was not sufficient to over-ride God's will or purpose for the man's life. The man would have needed to choose suicide to die—it would not be the will of the demons—and the man chose life. And when he saw Life coming, he ran toward him.

Other stories show a similar pattern. For example, Luke 4:31–37 shows a demon-oppressed man, and yet the demon did not/could not run away from Jesus. The passage even suggests that the man came to hear Jesus preach despite the demon's influence (vv. 31–33)! The demon threw him down, but did no harm (v. 35). The influence, while intense, had clear limits. Again, in Mark 9:14–29, the demon had a huge destruc-tive hold on the boy's life, yet it was not constant (v. 18) and it was not able to kill (destroy) him (v. 22). Elsewhere, Matt 9:32 tells of a demon who could only stop a man from speaking, and in Matt 12:22 a man was blind and mute. While these disabilities are significant, one does not see the torment associated with the previous stories, and they were pre-sented to Christ for healing without battles or resistance.

It would appear, therefore, not unreasonable to wonder if the limits placed upon the activities of the demons were in some way set by the ones oppressed. All demons would want the very worst for the possessed person, so anyone oppressed by a demon would exhibit the severest subjugation imaginable. Yet in these stories there is huge difference in impact. The only real variable in the equation would appear to be the individual themselves. Therefore, if the person consistently resisted the influence, would that minimise the impact upon their life? It would seem so, and one final story supports this idea—Paul's experience of the thorn in the side.

Paul's thorn is called a messenger (Gk, *angellos*) of Satan (2 Cor 12:7–9; cf. Job 2:7). This is the same word used for an angel, indicating that it may well have been a demonic angel attacking him. Paul was be-ing oppressed by demonic activity in order to hinder his gospel mission, the oppression being either physically, mentally, or spiritually shown. God's response to Paul's request for its removal was that his grace was sufficient to overcome the (evil) angelic influence, and that Satan's mes-senger would not win.

If an evil angel could have such an impact on Paul's life, yet not so much as to override God's grace or Paul's mission, could one then say that an individual's walk with God shapes the impact a demon has on one's life? If so, one might then reflect on what parallel good a holy angel may have. Just think of what might happen if a holy angelic influence cooperated with the grace and will of God alongside the human will. Consider what a powerful impact that would have one someone's life!

It seems that while angelic influence can be life changing, in the ultimate analysis it is limited. Exactly where those limits are is not clear. However, it appears that angelic influence needs our human will to agree with it to take actions of destiny-shaping proportions, while seemingly needing less cooperation for more life shaping implications.[18] Angels, therefore, are able to influence our lives, but we are still able ignore or resist their prompts or stirrings.

APPLYING A PASTORAL UNDERSTANDING OF THE ANGELS TO US

There are two main ways that a pastoral angelology theology can be applied to our lives. People are either touched or impacted by the angels directly, or a human pastor can encourage somebody with the truths about the ministry of angels. Both are valid and can work together.

First is a direct meeting with, or ministry from an angel. Stories of these kinds abound both in Scripture and throughout church history. We see an angel meeting with Gideon, a nervous man with little courage or faith, and he is guided and encouraged in what he should do (Judg 6:11–16). Similarly, Gabriel comes to Mary to prepare her for what was to come (Luke 1:26ff.), and an angel warns Joseph in a dream to leave for Egypt (Matt 2:13). For these people, the encounter was profound, and life changing, both for themselves and others.

Second is the personal encouragement of hearing, or being taught about, angels. One hears many stories of people who are lost or in trouble, with their hope ebbing. Suddenly they find a stranger appears and provides the perfect help, at the right time, in order to solve the apparently insurmountable problem. Some people realise it was an angel at the time, others come to that conclusion later, and others, I am sure, never realise it at all. These powerful testimonies can be a huge encouragement to people. It tells them that God, today, sees their predicaments, and when they need help the most, he will meet them in their time of need.

---

18. Thomas Aquinas comes to a similar conclusion, but via different route—cf. *ST* 1a:Q 110–11.

Alternatively, somebody maybe frightened by the prospect of death. The panic, fear, and hopelessness induced by this can be paralyzing. Alongside telling them about the love of God and the assurance of salvation in Jesus, you can also tell them of the truth of Luke 16:22, that angels will bear the soul of the believer to the bosom of Abraham.[19] Take heart! Your soul will not get lost on the way!

Finally, one should remember that some areas will overlap, and a neat division of cause and effect is not always possible. One act can impact on a person or situation in many ways. You cannot simply delineate angelic action and ministry into monochrome and singular events. One must recognise the wider, deeper, and more organic spiritual effects which can occur. An example would be angels removing demonic oppression, which will be discussed later. This not only brings freedom to the person, but is also an act of healing, of sustaining and preservation, and it demonstrates ongoing protection and blessing in life. This then allows you to move toward the goal that God has for you. In addition, it encourages others who see the release and freedom, and that God is active and blessing his people. One act; many possible effects.

Now we have a structure by which we can examine pastoral angelology, the rest of the book will explore the four areas of healing, sustaining, guidance, and reconciliation, starting with the place of angels in the life of Jesus himself.

19. The term "Abraham's bosom" is not common, nor is it clear what it exactly means. However, as Morris notes, is clearly suggests "felicity," and is directly contrasted with "Hades" for the rich man (Morris, *Luke*, 276). It also speaks of a place of intimacy, honor, and "paradisal blessing" (Green, *Luke*, 607).

4

Angels in the Life of Jesus

Now we should consider how angels were a part of Jesus' life and ministry, since if they played no role for him they would surely have no role with us. Alternatively, if they played a large role for him, so might they for us. So, what do we see? It seems to be an echo of Heb 1:14. Angels punctuate the Gospel accounts at regular and important points, playing a variety of roles, as a normal part of Jesus' life and thought.

Angels are present throughout and around-about the life and ministry of Jesus, but you should remember that the plain Gospel accounts would not have been his only experience of them. Prior to the incarnation, Jesus, as the Second Person of the Trinity, would have had personal experience of angels both in heaven and on earth. As their Creator God, he would have known exactly what substance and nature they were; how they lived, acted, and thought, and how their society was ordered; he would have watched them fall and then drag humanity down with them; and he would have been acutely aware of what he then had to do to put things right—the incarnation and the cross. In addition, if one accepts that some of the angelic appearances in the Old Testament were forms of theophanies of Christ, this experience would have been very real, personal, and practical.[1] Therefore Jesus could speak with authority about both realms and about angels and their ministry. So what do we see in the Gospels?

First we should note that we see no discussions about their creation, nature, fall, or organisation, amongst other traditional categories—even though Jesus would know all the answers to these questions. Jesus has no interest in scholastic categories, and never wonders how many angels can dance on the head of a pin! Alternatively, what we see is practical, and focussed on what they do, not who they are. It is also worth noting that

---

1. Theophanies, christophanies, and the Angel of the Lord will be discussed at the end of this chapter.

the place that the Gospels give to angels mirrors closely contemporary Jewish belief, especially in terms of their protection and guardianship of the godly.

From the outset angels were a part of the process for paving the way to the incarnation and Christ's subsequent ministry. Angels provided preparation and protection even before his conception and birth. When the angel came and met Zechariah to tell of the promise of a miracle for Elizabeth, God was using Gabriel to prepare the way for Christ, because John the Baptist would be Christ's forerunner, and the angel prepared his parents for this. Gabriel told them what John should be called, how he should be raised, and how he was to live.[2] This was a crash course in parenting. John would not be just a prophet of God, but *the* Prophet, for he would be instrumental in the early stages of Christ's own mission. Zechariah and Elizabeth were to bring up John as the angel directed. (Luke 1:13–17).

Gabriel then continued the mission and met with Mary, to prepare her for what was to happen. The gentle way in which Gabriel told Mary about what was to come, put her at ease. She accepted the word God had sent to her (Luke 1:26ff). Remember, this must have been an incredible shock, not only the visitation, but the mission as well—shaking Mary to her very core, but the angel guided her through it successfully. This gift of pastoral communication was equally evident when the angel spoke with Joseph about not divorcing Mary. Joseph had been in a quandary, wondering whether he should marry Mary (Matt 1:19–25). These meetings with the angel gave both Joseph and Mary, the strength to face the ridicule and scandal which probably dogged them throughout their marriage. The words of the angel were the visible sign from God, a lasting, physical memory, that what they did was right in his eyes, even if not in the society around them.

While the angel could, in both these circumstances, have just issued a blunt "Thus saith the LORD, . . ." and told them to get on with it, he did not. His presence might have suggested this, but nevertheless, he spoke and conversed with Mary and Joseph, setting them at ease with the unique situation, and assured them that the birth, and Jesus' formative years would be within a loving and whole family unit.

The next event is when the angel came to shepherds, with the glory of the LORD. Naturally this scared them, but the angel put them

---

2. Luke 1:5–25. This echoes the guidance the Angel of the Lord gave Samson's parents (Judg 13:1–14).

at ease—"Do not be afraid!" The angel explained what had happened, and where they were to go. Then a great company of the heavenly host appeared, and praised God, with a message that touched both heaven and earth—to which the shepherds respond that the *Lord* (not an angel) had spoken to them (Luke 2:8–15). Angels can represent and speak the very words of God, to the point that humans make no distinction between the messenger's word and the words of the one who sent him. Thinking beyond the worship, glory, and guidance, it is worth seeing that the angels were happy to relay the joyful news to one of the lowest classes of people. There is no pride for the angels, and they are willing to speak God's words to anybody, and guide them to the Savior.

The story of the early years of Jesus' life is completed with an act of protection. An angel appeared to Joseph in a dream to tell him to take the family to Egypt for their own protection, away from Herod's slaughter (Matt 2:19–21). Although the angel could have stood guard to save them from harm, he did not, but gave them an escape route instead. Angels do not leave God's people unprotected, or to fend for themselves, nor did they leave the job uncompleted. Angels may not always do the work for us, or act as we might expect. As God directed them, they did their job.

Angels, therefore, were integral to the successful negotiation of the early and vulnerable years of Jesus, being part of preparing the way to the birth, and then helping to protect him in childhood. But it did not stop there, since their ministry and presence continued into his adult years. After his baptism and affirmation by his Father, Jesus entered the wilderness for forty days of fasting and testing (Matt 4:1–11.Mark 1:12–13; Luke 4:1–13). One of the tests revolved around Ps 91:11–12, and how Jesus answered is important. Satan says: "If you are the Son of God, throw yourself down, for it is written, 'He will command his angels concerning you,' and 'On their hands they will bear you up, lest you strike your foot against a stone.' Jesus said to him, 'Again it is written, "You shall not put the Lord your God to the test."'" Jesus does not deny that angels would, could, and do come to protect. He and his family already had firsthand experience that they do! No, and as he later states, he could call upon twelve Legions to protect him (Matt 26:53). The point here is that removing people from artificially-created crises is not the realm in which angels operate. Angels respond to situations which result from obedient service to God, and they are sent as the simple and undeserved gift by the grace of God. Angels are not at our beck and call.

Satan then disappeared, and angels came to minister to Jesus—not at his bidding, but sent by the Father. This was an immediate demonstration of Jesus' point—angels do come, yet not at our demand, but from the love of the Father. That angels could minister to him shows the power and effectiveness of angelic ministry. Bear in mind, Jesus was the sinless God-man, yet even he benefited from their presence and ministry. The word here for "ministering" (Matt 4:11—*diēkonoun* / διηκονουν; cf. Mark 1:13) is rooted directly in *diakonian* / διακονιαν which is used in Heb 1:14. This, as we have seen, shows that what angels did for Jesus parallels what they do for his people in his church.

From this point onward, Jesus never calls upon the assistance of his angels, even though it was his right to do so. Nevertheless, angels permeated his teaching and still, one more time, they came to assist him in his hour of need, sent by the Father to support his beloved Son.

Angels appear in all four Gospels, punctuating Christ's teaching on a regular basis. It is worth considering how "off the cuff" some of his comments were. He assumed that those listening knew and agreed with what he was saying. Other times, it almost feels like the trump card in his argument, to which no one could respond. Angels and their ministry are simply not up for discussion. One listens and then either accepts or rejects. But to reject would be to reject Jesus' whole presentation at that time. Angels are naturally a part of what Jesus spoke about, and cannot be divorced from his teaching, or himself.

The Gospels show angels as God's agents, but also sets them firmly in the context of servants of Christ—as affirmed by Heb 1. This starts in John 1. The significance of Jesus speaking of Jacob's Ladder (John 1:51) is that while the initial vision in Gen 28 was incredible and pointed to a wider and greater reality, Jesus was superior to this. The story ends in Gen 28 with Jacob's statement that because the angels went up and down the ladder, "God is in this place . . . It is the house of God . . . a gateway to heaven" (Gen 28:16–17). The angelic presence showed the presence of God in that location (Bethel), and then angels showed it again, that God was in that place—in Jesus. Yes, heaven and earth are linked, and angels move between the two realms effortlessly and constantly, but Christ will link heaven and earth in a far superior way to that which angels can offer. Does this then mean that angels are now redundant, since it is the presence of the angels that point to the greater reality? No, the angels were at the bottom of the ladder as well as the top, and moving both up and down. Angels are still here, and angelic ministry continues under Christ, but it is now placed within a proper and wider context beneath Christ, who is God.

This is echoed in John 5:1–17 and the Pool of Bethsaida. Every so often God would send an angel to stir the pool, and a miraculous healing would happen. Jesus never contests this, and the fact that people would come, even wait for thirty-eight years, suggests there was more than something to the story. However, the people had to wait for the angel to come, and as the story indicates, many never had a chance to enter the pool anyway (v. 7). God entering the world and bringing healing via his angels was intermittent. However, through God in Jesus, healing was available here and now (cf. v. 17) and the healing was immediate, as it is shown to be throughout the Gospels. Everybody Jesus met who asked him for healing, he healed. And again, when God spoke to Jesus audibly (John 12:28–29), it was mistaken for an angel's voice. Heaven breaks into the earthly present, but it is God who does so now for his Son.

Another theme for Jesus is the association of angels and the coming judgement. While angels are not told when it will happen—God limits their knowledge of it—nevertheless they are to be his agents in the climax of history (Mark 13:32). In Matt 13:37–43 we have the parable of the weeds explained. There the angels are reapers (v. 39) gathering in wheat and weeds (which symbolise people). Fascinatingly, in v. 41, angels are said, by Jesus himself, to gather all *causes of sin* or *stumbling blocks*, as well as law breakers. These are two distinct groupings. The second is obviously people, but the first is described in the Greek with a neuter, and every use of this phrase in the Bible (including the LXX) refers to things or actions, not people (cf. Ps 140:9).[3] It also has echoes in other verses in Matthew, most importantly for us 18:6–7 (cf. 5:29; 7:23), which leads into the warning not to cause children to stumble because their angels see God's face.

Some commentators try to personalize the neuter, so both clauses can then refer to people, meaning angels only remove external physical obstacles such as people, and nothing internal to an individual. However, Leon Morris, recognising the neuter, rightly says it speaks of *the things that trap people and lead them into captivity to sin*.[4] Other scholars also see that the phrase echoes back to Zeph 1:3 which speaks of the *rubble/*

3. Luz, *Matthew*, 269.

4. Morris, *Matthew*, 357.

idols of the wicked (ESV), which points to idols (false gods, the worship of which shaped religious and social practices that displeased God), which cause sin, being removed. Carson notes this, and says that the phrase suggests stumbling blocks and offenses, means *things*, but can also include people.[5] The text is difficult to unravel, but the phrasing suggests that angels have the ability to remove not only people who cause sin, but also to somehow remove the internal effects of bad teaching or influence. This, once again, echoes back to the discussion in chapter 3 on how angels can influence people, since this verse indicates an angelic ability to work on us internally, correcting beliefs and attitudes (even though this instance specifically relates to what angels will do at the end of the age, there is no reason, given the wider biblical evidence, to believe that this ability is one solely given in the end times).

Therefore, Jesus sends (and comes with) his angels, and they will separate evil (people and things) from the righteous, and the evil people and *things* will be cast into the fire. Jesus will come in the glory of his Father with his angels (Matt 16:27), and he will send forth his angels (Matt 24:31) to gather his chosen/elect from the four corners of the earth. (The additional mention of "heavens" is probably hyperbole indicating that nobody can escape, and nowhere will be hidden from his angels during this event.) Angels have been given the insight to distinguish the righteous from the unrighteous, and the saved from unsaved, and they will get every decision right as they do their sifting—another indicator of the angelic ability to see within our hearts and minds and act according to what they find. Angels will serve Jesus at the sharp end of history (cf. Matt 25:31ff.; Mark 13:27). Angels do their job well, and complete it.

Finally, the more personal description of angels and their relationship to humans is often mentioned by Jesus. Jesus does not present angels as detached, inscrutable beings who one day in the future will come in judgement. He speaks of them as personal beings with feelings and emotions, who care about humanity in the way he does.

In the parable of Poor Lazarus and the Rich Man (Luke 16:19–31), when Lazarus dies, after what seems to be miserable life, the angels take him to Abraham's side—in stark contrast to the rich man who was merely buried (Luke 16:22). Here we sense Jesus sneaking in a passing comment, which actually holds huge meaning. Picture the scene—

5. Carson, *Matthew*, 326.

the holy angels carrying a filthy beggar to heaven. There is an incredible richness about the picture. Angels (plural) came, almost like an escort or cortège of honor, to take the lowly one to heaven, and as we know angels never fail or get their task wrong.

At times, Jesus' words are resonant of the idea of the heavenly council found in the Old Testament, a council which takes an interest in the affairs of humanity (Job 1; Jer 23:18–22). For example, in Luke 12:8–9, Jesus says he will acknowledge before angels all those who acknowledge him, and likewise disown before the angels those who reject him (cf. Luke 9:26; Mark 8:38). This idea resurfaces later in Luke 15:10 where there is joy and celebration in the presence of the angels over the repentance of one sinner. Angels observe events on earth, and have an opinion about them. And when what they see is good, they rejoice! The angels, collectively, are concerned with the spiritual welfare of people, and Matt 18:10 makes this point well. Following on from discussions around who is the greatest in the kingdom of heaven, Jesus calls a child to him, and the child becomes the model for true greatness (Matt 18:2–3). (Children were of low social standing or status, and totally dependent on their parents.) Humility (Matt 18:4), and receiving children in his name (Matt 18:5) marks out greatness. One must not cause the lowly to stumble (Matt 18:6–7), and should take drastic measures to ensure this is so (Matt 18:8–9). Why? "See that you do not look down on one of these little ones. For I tell you that their angels in heaven always see the face of my Father in heaven." This comment is made without defence or apology, and echoes Jesus' wider teaching about angels. Angels have no fear or dislike of the lowly, in fact the angels stand before God in heaven and discuss with the Father these lowly ones. Returning again to the imagery of heavenly court, you cannot imagine that God's angelic council, before whom people will/will not be acknowledged, and who will gather the elect and take them to Abraham's bosom, would be silent as the lowly ones are abused or caused to stumble.

Finally, we must consider the question concerning the seven husbands for one woman, where Jesus' reply to the Sadducees makes a point wider than the nature of the resurrection body and state. (Sadducees, as we have noted, rejected the idea of the spiritual realm, bodily resurrection, and angels as popularly understood by most first century Jews.) After listening to this convoluted story, Jesus says to them, "You are in error. You do not know the Scriptures or God's power

. . . Have you not read what God has said to you?" (Matt 22:29, 31). What is it they should have known? Jesus tells them that in the resurrection people will be *like the angels* (Matt 22:29–31) The parallel in Luke 20:36 is slightly different and potentially much stronger, having the possible meaning of not only like, but *equal to the angels*.[6] Quite what this may mean will be examined later, but it is noteworthy that it is within the context of a comment where Jesus questions whether the Sadducees know their Scripture, since this truth has eluded them so comprehensively. A developed understanding of angels was, unless you were a Sadducee, taken for granted as a part of the worldview (and heaven-view, if you like!) of many Jews, and Jesus freely mentioned and cited angels and their ministry without defence, apology, or embarrassment. Furthermore, he expected the listeners to know what he was saying. In fact, when it comes to the Sadducees, Jesus clearly challenges and rejects their position—which should cause food for thought for those Christians who do not believe in angels, as well as those whose theology effectively have angels as a non-applied theory. Angels regularly punctuate Jesus' speeches, sermons, and seemingly off-the-cuff observations. Angels are naturally present throughout Jesus' teaching, as ones living alongside, active within, and loving of, his creation.

We now arrive at Gethsemane (Luke 22:39–46), the point in Christ's life where he is asking, and facing, the most difficult questions. And in this hour of need, who stands with him there? His disciples are falling asleep and he appears to be alone. Yet in the Father's mercy, Jesus is sent an angel. Jesus does not ask for this, but one comes nevertheless, and once again it is worth noting that he is the incarnate Jesus. The God-man truly and really benefitted from the angel's ministry to him. The text said he was strengthened by the angel (v. 43: *eniskuōn* / ενισχυων). This is not the word used in connection with the temptation in Matt 4:11 and Mark 1:13. It has the literal meaning of imparting strength. It does not mean strengthen in the sense of encouraging and spurring on—a purely mental building up. It is a physical word to *give and impart strength* and it led to Jesus having the physical stamina to pray further.

It is used again by Luke in Acts 9:19 when Paul, after three days without food, ate a meal and was physically strengthened and revived. This is also the case in 1 Kgs 19:8 (LXX) when an angel fed Elijah to

---

6. Matt 22:30 says "like the angels" (*hos angelloi* / ως αγγελοι). Luke 20:36 says, "equal unto the angels" (*isangelloi* / ισαγγελοι). A fuller discussion of this will come in ch. 8.

prepare him for his long journey ahead, and Elijah was strengthened. Similarly, the word is used in Dan 8:18 and 10:8–10 (LXX) when Daniel met an angel and then the fiery figure, and collapsed at the sight. The angel touched him, as the fiery figure did later, and Daniel's strength returned, enabling him to stand up again.

So, an angel imparted physical strength to Jesus to continue his task and to mission, and this reflects our discussion about how angels minister. As a demon can give strength to break chains, so an angel can work within the human body to give extra strength to pray and carry on.

At this point both angels and disciples leave. Jesus faces his trial and death alone. One cannot imagine that the angels were unaffected by what they saw, but while they could have stopped the horror, they did not act, since to do so would contravene the will of the Father. So they watched, as the Father did, I would surmise, in unspeakable sadness.

After Jesus died and was laid in the tomb, we next see angels there to meet Mary and the concern and pastoral tone of their conversation is clear. What is also clear is their commission to Mary to go and tell the others that Jesus had been raised from the dead (Matt 28:5–8; Mark 16:6–7; Luke 24:10) In Matthew's account (Matt 28:1–8), the women came to the tomb, and an angel of the Lord descended, accompanied by an earthquake, and rolled back the stone. His clothes were like lightning and white as snow, which fits with various Old Testament descriptions. Naturally this was frightening, for the soldiers and the women, yet the angel said to women (note, not the soldiers), "Do not fear!" The angel then explained the situation, telling them to come and see the empty tomb, and then go and tell the disciples, since Jesus will be in Galilee (Matt 28:5–7). It is worth reflecting here on the similarity of this situation to Mary and Joseph's. They were faced with huge, life changing events beyond human comprehension, but the situation and then the commissioning, were all successfully negotiated by the angel. The angel spent time speaking to the women, so while they felt afraid, yet they were filled with joy when they left—the angel was able to put them at ease and send them on their way, commissioned, and with the information they required. This angelic attestation of the resurrection and commission of the women was not insignificant, as is affirmed by Luke, when the two on the Emmaus Road spoke of those women who had seen a vision of angels who said Jesus was alive (Luke 24:23). This was news and further authentication of the resurrection.

Acts 1:10-11 shows the last time angels would be with Jesus on earth—until the Second Coming. A feature here, which recurs through Acts, is for the angels to re-orientate and refocus the eyes of the disciples back to the task in hand—spreading the gospel and telling people about Jesus. "Why do you stand here looking at the sky?" the angels ask them. Didn't Jesus say he would return as he left? The force of the initial part of the statement is clear—"Don't just stand there, get on with it!" Angels, again, spur the believers into action, to spread the gospel and message of Christ.

Finally, we see the angels living and worshipping in heaven, with Christ, as shown in the book of Revelation. We will look at this later, but the joy, unity and the focus of the angels upon doing God's will upon the earth is clear. From start to finish, Jesus and the angels are friends, but the angels are also his servants and they do his will—just as we humans are, and should do.

THE ANGEL OF THE LORD

While not something mentioned within the New Testament, the relationship between Jesus and the enigmatic Old Testament figure of the Angel of the LORD became a common question for later Christian theologians. We have seen that Jesus valued angels and their ministry, but some early Christians looked back into the Old Testament and made a stronger link between Christ and this Angel, arguing that they were one and the same. Therefore to complete our discussion about Jesus and angels, one needs to ask, "Who is the being named as *the Angel of the LORD*?" Is it God appearing in angelic form (a theophany), Christ appearing in angelic form (a christophany), or just an angel? This is important, since if the ministry and work of the Angel of the LORD is in fact the activity of *God himself*, then one would need be very cautious if citing them as a case of straightforward angelic ministry.

The precise identity of the Angel of the LORD is not given, in either Old or New Testaments. However, we do have some clues. There are references to "angels of the Lord," "*an* angel of the Lord," and "*the* angel of the Lord," but it seems that when the definite article—"the"—is used, it is specifying a unique being, different from other angels. The Angel of the LORD sometimes speaks *as* God, sometimes *identifies himself with* God, and sometimes exercises the responsibilities of God. The Angel is also worshipped because Yahweh is present (e.g., Josh 5:14). Since angels are not God and therefore stop people worshipping them (Rev 19:10; 22:8), for one to allow worship, means it must be God. And since the role the Angel plays is often one of rescue, then naturally a link is built with God as Savior. Yet the Angel is also spoken *to* by God, and is shown as *distinct from* God. In some of these appearances, those who saw the Angel of the LORD feared for their lives because they had "seen the Lord."[7] Therefore, it is reasonable to believe that in at least some instances, the Angel of the LORD is a christophany. The appearances of the Angel of the LORD then cease after the incarnation of Christ, and it is never mentioned in the New Testament. It is possible, therefore, that the appearances of the Angel of the LORD were manifestations of Jesus before his incarnation— christophanies. Jesus declared himself to be existent "before Abraham" (John 8:58), so it is possible that he would be active and manifest in the world before his incarnation (cf. John 12:41).

Whether the Angel is specifically Christ, or is a more general theophany, he has a number of close parallels with God. However, there are some problems, which call for caution when trying to make a blanket assertion of this kind.

1. The use of the term is not consistent, either across the Old Testament, or within individual books/writers. For example, the pillar of cloud is variously called *an* angel (Exod 23:20; 33:2), *my* angel (Exod 23:23; 32:34), and *the* angel (Exod 14:19). Also, in 1 Kgs 19, the angel who ministered to Elijah is called both *the* (v. 7) and *an* (v. 5) angel of the LORD. A similar inconsistency in use is shown throughout Zechariah.

2. An angel is able to carry God's Name, without always being able to do what one would expect God to do. The pillar of cloud is said to carry God's name, literally, *in-within-him* (Exod 23:21). The significance of carrying God's name is clear, but what that actually means is not. There is a status and authority uniquely conferred, given and shared, but does this mean that God's very nature is also conferred? Some commentators would say so, others see this as problematic and so do not make that direct and simple link. For if the Angel carries the name (and thus nature), then it could do what God does. Yet it cannot. Bruckner

7. Main texts concerning the Angel of the Lord—Gen 16:7–12; 21:17–18; 22:11–18; Exod 3:2; Judg 2:1–4; 5:23; 6:11–24; 13:3–22; 2 Sam 24:16; Zech 1:12; 3:1; 12:8.

makes the point well: "The Name in the angel means that the angel was powerful and effective, but as a messenger, not capable of forgiving rebellion. The people would rebel against the angel's guidance in 32:23, and the Lord had to intervene to forgive (Exod 34:6–7)."[8] God forgave—the Angel did not—which is strange if the Angel was God. Carrying God's name was not synonymous with carrying God's ability to forgive. Similarly, the Angel, while carrying his name, did not carry God's presence. God refused to go with the people (Exod 33:3), but the Angel did go, which was why Moses asked for God to be present as well (Exod 33:12ff.). With no presence present, no theophany is possible, yet this lack of divine presence can coexist with the presence of the Angel carrying the divine name. Bruckner concludes by saying: "The angel was not the Lord, but would deliver the guidance and protection of the Lord . . . [It is worth noting that] in the end Moses' conversations were always directly with the Lord and never with the angel."[9] The Angel always stood outside the Tent while Moses went inside to speak with God. Moses did not speak with the Angel face to face, but with God. If the Angel were God, Moses would have spoken to him.

Therefore, one could call the Angel by the name it carries internally—God's name, Yahweh—yet this need not necessarily translate into the presence of God being there in the Angel, as a theophany would demand. This would make sense of those times when the Angel was sometimes called "Lord," when its actions suggested it might not be.

3.   Furthermore, God can empower an angel to do a task he himself usually does, without a theophany occurring. The clearest example of this would be in Isa 6, where the angelic being is the vehicle by which God forgives and cleanses Isaiah. God himself does not do it directly, but uses the angel to enact it by action and word. A classic example of God using angels as *secondary means* (see chapter 8 on *Reconciliation*). With this is mind, when one looks at the work of cleansing the Angel of the LORD does in Zech 3, one is not required to say that the Angel cleansed

8. Bruckner, *Exodus*, 220.
9. Ibid.

and therefore is God. Isa 6 shows that God can give angels the authority to do this on his behalf without also giving his nature as well.

4.   Flowing from this point, the Angel of the LORD is said to speak God's words, which suggests that it is God himself speaking. However, an angel, as God's messenger, can speak on behalf of God and so literally speak God's words. In the cultures of the time, the words of a king's messenger were treated as if it were the king himself speaking. And the Bible itself shows us there is no anomaly between angels speaking and also conveying God's direct words. In Luke 2 an angel of the LORD came and spoke to the shepherds, telling them of the wonderful things that God was doing, and about Jesus (Luke 2:9). The shepherds recognised that "The Lord had made these things known to them" (Luke 2:15). Clearly, God had not told them, an angel had (not even *the* Angel, but just *an* angel) conveyed his message. And it could not have been a christophany since Jesus was lying in a manger a few miles away. There was no theophany here, yet the angel's words are said to be the words of the LORD. A similar thing is shown in Exod 23:22 where God, indicating that the pillar of cloud is his literal mouthpiece, says "If you listen carefully to what [the angel] says, and do all that I say." Therefore, the Bible does not always make the direct, hard and fast link between the one who speaks and the one who sends the speaker.

5.   Flowing from this is that there is nothing that demands every appearance of the Angel is actually of the same angel—that there is only one Angel of the LORD. There are many groups of angels named in Scripture, and there is no reason why there might not be one group of angels, from which God calls one into service, and when he appears is named the Angel. Is it a single person or indicative of a broader category, like, for example, who is *the* captain of England's football team? That depends on when you ask the question. It is a singular role, with a singular title, that different people can fill at different times. The term "the Angel of the LORD" could simply designate a role which different angels could enact, and which the LORD himself chose to step into

sometimes. It is not clear, especially in the light of the difficulties noted above, that it is the self same angel each time.

6. One cannot see the face of God and live, yet people did see the LORD's angel and live (Exod 33:20; cf. Gen 32:30; Jdg 6:22).

7. If Jesus is the Angel of the LORD, it was he who was going to destroy Jerusalem, and who massacred 185,000 Assyrians (Isa 37:36; cf. 2 Sam 24:16). While Jesus has the power of judgement in his hands (e.g., Matt 25:31–34, 41, 46; Acts 10:42; 2 Thess 1:5–10), for some, these accounts do not sit that neatly with the New Testament picture of him.

8. Finally, while New Testament writers are very keen to see Old Testament pictures of Christ—to cite and clearly apply various prophecies and Scriptures to him—it is striking that this link is never made with regards to the Angel of the LORD. Similarly, Jesus never makes the link to himself either. It looks like a typological gift, a wide open goal ready to be taken, yet it never is. And for all the other links to be noted and for this one not to be suggests that the New Testament writers did not recognise the connection. The book of Hebrews is a case in point. After a discussion about the place of Jesus and the angels, and saying that Christ was present at the time of the Exodus, here was the prime opportunity to clarify and make the clear connection and say Jesus was the Angel in the pillar of cloud, or Jesus was the Angel of the LORD. Yet the writer does not. Christ was clearly said, by numerous writers, and by himself, to have been present and active in the Old Testament (cf. 1 Cor 10:4), but never is he linked to the Angel of the LORD or, for example, the pillar of cloud, despite the opportunities to do so.

This last point is crucial, and should control any assumptions, theology, and reading of texts around the Angel of the LORD. To take such a step as to make a straight and simple identification of the Angel of the LORD with Christ is to do so without any New Testament support. The New Testament has 343 direct Old Testament quotations, plus over 2,000 verbal allusions and parallels.[10] Not one of these mentions the Angel of the LORD, and none make any direct link, nor even any vague attempt

---

10. Motyer, "Old Testament in the New Testament."

to. This is not shown to be in the thinking of any New Testament writers who met, knew and spoke with Christ himself. However, this does not mean that the idea is totally without premise. I fully agree that in some instances there is a clear theophany (as opposed to Christophany), especially when the Angel is worshipped, or self-identifies as God. I would therefore say the following are theophanies:

- Gen 18–19: Of the three angelic figures who met Abraham, one clearly stands out from the others, and exercises the power and authority of God (esp. 18:10; cf. 21:1).

- Gen 22: Abraham and Isaac. The angel said Abraham "did not withhold your son from *me*." Distinct from just speaking God's words, the angel self identifies as God.

- Gen 31:11–13: The Angel of the LORD self indentifies as God, and said, "*I am* the God of Bethel."

- Gen 32:30: Jacob wrestling the man said he saw God face to face. But this is only called an angel in a much later writing (Hos 12:4).

- Exod 3:2–4: The angel was said to be in the bush, and God was in the bush, and God called to Moses from the bush. The ground was also holy, which parallels Josh 5:13–15.

- Josh 5:13–15: The Commander of the LORD's army was worshipped, and the ground where he was, was holy.

- Judg 13: The Angel of the LORD met with Samson's parents, but Samson's father said, "I have seen the LORD," in a similar way to Jacob in Gen 32. However, it is only the identification by Samson's father that suggests that the angel was Yahweh.

As for the other examples, I believe none are clearly theophanies. Yet this is not to say that some might not be. However, a proper and full biblical angelology would allow for the possibility that all the others were simply encounters with a specially commissioned angel.

Now we have seen how angels were involved in the life of Christ, allied to our deeper understanding of Hebrews 1:14, we can now ask: What does a pastoral and applied theology of angels look like, and what has it got to do with us?

～ 5

ANGELS AND HEALING

IN A BROKEN WORLD full of broken people, the need for healing of all kinds is not only desirable but a necessary starting point for any spiritual journey and relationship with God. A cripple cannot walk the road until their legs are made strong enough to do so. The blind cannot see the path until their sight is restored. The first step with God must be that of healing, and as we saw earlier, healing is an event, or series of events, or a process) in one's life which promotes physical and spiritual wholeness.

While angels can be the *conduits* of God's healing presence, biblically, one must recognise that God is the only source of all healing. Therefore, strictly speaking, angels cannot and do not heal. However, in the same way that humans have skills and gifts for healing (as do doctors), or be ones through whom God does miraculous healing, as we see the disciples and apostles do in the Gospels and Acts,[1] so can angels. Alongside this direct involvement, is the more indirect activity of, for example, angels as ones who stand alongside us to lead us into a position or place where God can heal us directly.

How do angels help us in this area? Clebsch and Jaekle note five ways that human ministers are involved in the ministry of healing. First is by anointing the sick person with oil (Jas 5:14–15), and by encouraging regular participation in the sacramental grace offered through the church. The second is by prayer, and to stand with the person in need and intercede to God on their behalf for healing. Third is what we may now call faith healing—the miraculous gift of the charismatic healer with special God-given healing powers. Fourth is exorcism where demonic oppression is removed, bringing release and wholeness. Finally

---

1. E.g., Matt 10:1; Acts 3:7–8; 5:16; 8:7; 14:9–10; cf. 1 Cor 12:9, 28.

is *magico-medicine*, which are the various superstitious charms, potions, and rituals people use to heal themselves.

Not all of these can be called biblical, and so angels would not be involved in all of them. However, we will see that angels are involved in healing in some of these ways. We shall see angels serving as conduits of God's grace and power, angels encouraging people to live the life of grace within the church, angels being involved in prayer, and angels being a part of fighting and removing demonic oppression.

ANGELS AS CONDUITS OF HEALING

As direct conduits of healing, angels can be involved in miraculous, divine intervention—incredible wonders and phenomena which in biblical times, caused amazement and awe. The miracles of Jesus, which the disciples and apostles were also gifted to do, not only lifted physical incapacity, oppression, and depression from people, but also made them reconsider both their lives and God.

Direct supernatural physical healing through angels is not common in Scripture, maybe because it really is the province of God, and mistaking creature for Creator in the realm of physical healing is not unknown. Just consider the reaction to Paul and Barnabas healing the crippled man—Paul was called Hermes, Barnabas Zeus, and people tried to sacrifice to them (Acts 14:8–13). Humans and angels both are prone to being misunderstood and/or worshipped if involved in healing and miracles. Probably in the light of other warnings about the worship of angels and the extreme reactions they can sometimes bring forth from the even most devout of people (Rev 22:8–9), this aspect of angelic ministry is not emphasised. However, this does not mean it is absent, and a more subtle involvement in healing is often pointed to, both openly miraculous and otherwise.

Taking what maybe called "miraculous" healings first, John 5:1–17 (esp. v. 5) is the most obvious example of this (see chapter 4). Little actual detail is given about how this worked with regard to the angels, but it is of interest how the story the plays out. Jesus, after healing the man (5:8), tells him plainly to stop sinning or something else worse would happen to him (5:14). This story suggests that while Jesus heals, angels can also be involved in healing, and that any healing should result in a changed life.

Consider Zechariah and Elizabeth in Luke 1:5–25. They were unable to have children, and whatever the problem, they were both old now. It was the encounter with the angel that God used as a vehicle for reversing that condition, and allowing conception to take place. This was not only a physical healing, but also what one might call a "social healing," since both the angelic visitation and subsequent pregnancy took away their shame and disgrace in the community, and showed God's direct blessing upon their lives (Luke 1:25).

However, healing can also be the provision of strength to overcome illness or infirmity. When you are ill or sick, you feel weakened and rundown. You need strength and energy to fight the sickness, and allow your body to recover. When physically drained and wanting to be revived, what we need among other things is the strength to recover. Angels can give people renewed physical strength and also strengthen those who are weak. We have already seen how an angel did this for Jesus in Gethsemane (Luke 22:43). The angel came and *gave* strength to him, reinvigorating him to continue praying in readiness for what was to come. When we are run down, angels can strengthen us to face the tasks, illnesses, and battles of life. This also happened when Daniel collapsed and the *fiery figure* touched him to raise him to his feet. Who this figure is is not clear; however what he did in Dan 10:8–10, is directly paralleled by Gabriel in Dan 8:18—Daniel was weak as if he was asleep, but Gabriel touched and revived him.

Therefore, while it rare to see an angel enact a supernatural healing, it is not excluded as a possibility. Far more likely is that when you are in a state of weakness and vulnerability, an angel can give you strength when you most need it, just as one did for Jesus in Gethsemane.

ANGELS AND BEING IN THE BODY OF CHRIST

Encouraging people not only to go to church but to live the life that God offers within the body of Christ is a clear way to place people within a situation conducive to healing. This is not to say that people outside the church or the people of God are not healed—the Bible is clear that this does happen, often to the chagrin of those who think it shouldn't (2 Kgs 5; cf. Luke 4:22–29; Mark 7:25–30). However, it is common sense to think that just as the best place for the healing a sick person is hospital, so the best place for spiritual healing is the church. And yes, the church is also a place where physical and emotional healing can happen. Angels drawing people to Christ and into the church is part of the wider healing process, and so it is no surprise that we see angels, alongside us, proclaiming the gospel to the world: "Then I saw another angel flying directly overhead, with an eternal gospel to proclaim to those who dwell on earth, to every nation and tribe and language and people" (Rev 14:6).

This area will be covered in far more depth in the chapter on guiding, but a specific example of this would be in Acts 5:18–21: "[The Jewish authorities] arrested the apostles and put them in the public prison. But during the night an angel of the Lord opened the prison doors and brought them out, and said, 'Go and stand in the temple and speak to the people all the words of this Life.' And when they heard this, they entered the temple at daybreak and began to teach."

Too often we focus on the miraculous angelic escape and forget what the angel then said. Coming out of jail, I would think the last thing on the apostles' minds was to go back into the lion's den—the temple—and start all over again. Yet they were told to do just that, and the angel called it preaching *Life*. Many commentators have said this is an odd term to use, but see a parallel in Acts 3:15, where Jesus is called the Author of Life. F. F. Bruce, though, sees the beauty and poetry behind the phrase, calling it "an apt term for the message of salvation."[2] Not just sin and salvation, but Life with a capital "L" (some translations miss this subtly, by just calling it "new life"). This, to me, is a wonderfully holistic and pastoral way of viewing salvation through Christ. And this is what angels call us to preach to the world.

Suffice to say that one of the consistent post-Pentecost activities of angels is to advance the gospel, by exhorting the apostles, especially in the face of opposition, to preaching, and focusing on telling the message of the Christ so that others might be saved. And so with us, while many forms of counselling and support are available to those around us, we may sometimes need an angel to prompt and refocus us to the fact that the best foundation for any pastoral care is Jesus Christ, and we must direct everybody, Christian or not, to this truth. Jesus is the Way, the Truth, and the Life, and Life is only found through him.

Yet for those who are already Christians, a slightly different tack may need to be taken. Classically, the church is the ark of salvation, where the saved people live together under Jesus. It is also where we are called

2. Bruce, *Acts*, 110.

to live, holy, whole and healthy lives. To be an active member of the body of Christ, you need a lifestyle and attitudes which draw you in and allow you to feed and be inspired. It is difficult to be spiritually nourished if you live a life which is spiritually self-destructive. The role of angels to inspire holy living is, implicitly, a call to a healthy Christian life alongside other Christians, which allows you to be touched by the grace that God lavishes upon his church. Angels bring words of encouragement, warning and guidance that direct people in how they should act and live.[3] The presence of angels also reminds us that we are on a stage. We live our lives before a heavenly audience, and so we should be aware of how act. We have already read how St. Paul in 1 Cor 11:10 demands proper order in church *because of the angels*, and the encouragement to holy living in 1 Tim 5:21, since we stand before both God and his angels. But for now, we can consider the call in 1 Cor 6:3: "Do you not know we will judge the angels?"

Christian brothers and sisters should act rightly toward each other, in a wise and godly way, and not, through malice and broken relationships. Because we will judge angels, we need to learn how to judge each other now, and bitterness and vengefulness toward fellow Christians is not the way to live. Reflecting on the angels and angelic life should lead us to consider our own ways, especially in relationship to others. And on this point, the fellowship between angels and humans is a beautiful relationship, which we should model to each other. This will be further discussed in the chapter on reconciliation, but we should consider how angels love and serve us, pleading for us before the face of the Father. And surely, if they do that for us, we should do it for our fellow brothers and sisters in Christ, and for non-Christians too? Our faith, like the trust of the angels in God, should be outwardly expressed, not inwardly turned.

We are to live in an obedient and godly manner because we are in front of other created beings who lived in an obedient and godly manner. Angels are held up as a standard to live by. Consider the angels and consider how they live under God, and then compare your own life to their obedience and holiness. Reordering life, leads you into a more holy life, which is a better place to receive healing, and angels can help us on that journey.

---

3. E.g., Gen 16:7–12; Gen 21:17; Luke 1:26–38; Acts 27:23–24.

ANGELS AND PRAYER

One of the most amazing things we are told in Scripture is that angels pray for us. Prayer touches upon every area of pastoral care and the Christian life, and will be fully discussed in chapter 6. However, that the Bible links prayer to healing is obvious, with Jesus making this exact point (e.g., Mark 9:17–29, esp. 29). But when considering prayer and healing, I am drawn to reflect on Jas 5:14–16: "Is anyone among you sick? Let him call for the elders of the church, and let them pray over him, anointing him with oil in the name of the Lord. And the prayer of faith will save the one who is sick, and the Lord will raise him up. And if he has committed sins, he will be forgiven. Therefore, confess your sins to one another and pray for one another, that you may be healed. The prayer of a righteous person has great power as it is working."

I will consider whether we should ask angels to pray for us in the next chapter, but for now we can note that angels (who not only would have the qualifications of elders,[4] but who surely would have a similar compassion for the sick) will pray over us in Jesus' name, and their prayers will raise up the sick person, restoring him/her to health. The Greek here has an interesting double echo. The word for "raise" or "heal" (v. 15) is *sōsei* / σωσει, which has the root of *sōzō* / σῴζω which means to be saved or rescued. It is also worth seeing here the link with forgiveness and confession. Clearly if one sees sin as a form of sickness or illness, so forgiveness and cleansing from sin is a part of the healing process. Isa 6:6–7 shows how angels are a part of this process, which is a healing in itself. Isaiah bewails and confesses his sin before both God on his throne and his angels: "Then one of the seraphim flew to me, having in his hand a burning coal that he had taken with tongs from the altar. And he touched my mouth and said: '*Behold, this has touched your lips; your guilt is taken away, and your sin atoned for.*'"

Clearly, angels do not forgive sin, and salvation is not found through angels. However, just as Christ gave the right to humans to pronounce forgiveness (Matt 18:18), and set them free from their burdens, we see forgiveness is declared and pronounced by the angel on behalf of

---

4. Glasscock, in *The Biblical Concept of Elder*, puts together an extensive list of personal, public, family, and ministry qualifications that a Christian leader needs. The two lists, from 1 Tim 3:1–7 and Titus 1:5–9 give at least twenty-two qualifications. A cursory glance at these lists would suggest that angels more than fulfil the ethical, spiritual, and personal criteria for an elder, with human family and social considerations excepted.

God, alongside the restorative action of touching Isaiah's lips. Angels, like humans, can effectually proclaim forgiveness in God's name. When forgiveness is declared, it is true and has happened, and this advances the healing journey. Mark Morton, reflecting on Ps 32:3–5 said: "By acknowledging our sin and confessing it we are recognising the problems, affirming our desire for change, and inviting the Holy Spirit to execute that change. The process of confession is therefore a process of healing through which we are reconciled to ourselves, to our neighbour and to the Lord."[5]

I know for myself acting in both a pastoral position and the position of the one confessing, to be told by a Christian who knows and loves you, "You have confessed. You are forgiven!" is truly powerful and profoundly releasing. Can you imagine how Isaiah felt when God sent his angel, and was told by this holy being *"Your guilt is taken away, and your sin atoned for!"*? Angels stand before the Father and see us, and they hear us when we pray. They encourage our repentance, they proclaim our repentance, and they rejoice as we repent, and they do all of this before the God of forgiveness. The angels' joy is heaven's joy at the lost sheep being found by God (Luke 15:3–7).

Angels are righteous (holy) beings, so their prayer is powerful and effective. I sometimes think that the angels praying for us, are the engine room of spiritual life. Many of us know that when a body of people pray for us, we can see and feel a tangible change in our life and circumstances. Angels pray unceasingly, from a pure and righteous relationship with God. As you are encouraged by a friend praying for you, so too should we be encouraged that angels are doing the same. What an honor to thank God for!

ANGELS AND DEMONIC OPPRESSION

How the removal of demonic oppression links into healing may not, at first glance, be obvious. But when one considers that the removal of demonic oppression is central to some of Jesus' healings, it begins to make far more sense. Luke 8 has the already discussed story of the healing of the demoniac and the casting of Legion into the pigs. How the story ends is of interest here:

---

5. Morton, *Personal Confession Reconsidered*, 6.

> When they came to Jesus, they found the man, from whom the demons had gone out, sitting at Jesus' feet, dressed and in his right mind . . . Those who had seen it told the people how the demon-possessed man had been cured . . . The man from whom the demons had gone out begged to go with him, but Jesus sent him away, saying, "Return home and tell how much God has done for you." So the man went away and told all over town how much Jesus had done for him. (Luke 8:35–39)

The man was now sane and acting calmly (full inner healing), and begging to go with Jesus. Jesus, however, tells him to go and speak to people of what had happened to him. Here is a removal of demonic oppression resulting in healing (the Greek word, again, has the dual sense of restoration and salvation (*sōzō*; cf. Acts 2:40, 47), wholeness, a desire to follow Jesus, and a willingness to speak of the wonders of God to others. Similarly, for example, Matt 9:32–33 tells of a demon cast out from a mute allowing him to speak, Mark 9:14–29 tells of a tormented boy healed by the exorcising of an unclean spirit, and Luke 13:10–16 has the crippled woman healed by the removal of Satan's oppression in her life.

Fighting demons, removing demonic oppression, and expelling evil spirits from peoples' lives can lead to healing and a new life following Jesus. Angels fight and defeat demons. It is natural, therefore, that this work they do would have an effect in the area of healing in peoples' lives.

The broad canvas of angels defeating demons is shown in Rev 12:7–12, where Michael and his angels defeat Satan and his demons, throwing them out of heaven. Demons cannot withstand the angelic army of God. The army is mighty and large, Jesus has twelve legions at his disposal (cf. Luke 2:13—multitude; Acts 7:42—host), and they fight for him. Even though Jesus is clearly the focus of the text, and Satan's defeat is the result of Christ's triumph, it is Michael who comes with his angels to fight. The heavenly warriors are not led into battle by Jesus, but Michael. It is worth stopping here and pondering this. Michael led the charge, not Jesus. This can only be because Jesus gave Michael the power and authority to fight this battle. (Another example of *secondary means*, perhaps.) Jesus empowered Michael (whose name means "one who is like God") for this task, a mighty task—perhaps Jesus even placed his Name in Michael (cf. Exod 23:21). And similarly, all angelic ministry starts and ends in the commission and empowerment of God, not within the angels' own being. Michael knew who was his Lord and God, and in whose name he was fighting. When fighting Satan, Michael knew where his authority came from. Jude 9 says: "But when the archangel Michael, contending with the devil, was disputing about the body of Moses, he did not presume to pronounce a blasphemous judgment, but said, 'The Lord rebuke you.'"

In the midst of battling Satan, Michael calls upon the name of the Lord as a rebuke to Satan. It was not of himself, but the Lord who rebukes and defeats Satan. Michael and his angels represent the heavenly victory of Christ, but they can only fight this battle because of Christ's triumph.[6] And Christ's triumph means Michael triumphs. Satan and his demons do not have what it takes to defeat the heavenly army, and they are cast down out of heaven. There is no place in heaven for Satan and his demons (Rev 20:11), and heaven becomes a demon-free zone, a place of peace which God's people will inhabit (Rev 21:4).

And yet, Satan, though defeated, is not to be disregarded. He is the great dragon, the serpent, the devil, who accuses the brethren. Satan is no fairy tale monster, but a real adversary, who has demons to help him. Satan continues to be troublesome and destructive, and so we need the help of God to stand against him. That Satan and his demons are cast down is significant. What St John indicates in Revelation is that what happens in heaven will have its parallel impact here in earth. Satan has been defeated, but he is here on earth, which explains why churches are suffering, and why Christians and non-Christians alike are tempted away and become dissatisfied, looking for secular power, security, and fulfilment. We are in a battle, as Paul tells us in Eph 6, and our foes are not flesh and blood, but demonic powers.

Yet, this is not whole picture. Leon Morris says, "John reminds us that the conflict is not simply one between demons and men. Angelic forces are also engaged."[7] Yes we are in a battle, but we are not alone. The victorious angels, under Christ, battle with us, and alongside us. The victory is assured. Skirmishes still happen, and casualties still sadly occur, but we can always call upon God to send his angels to fight for us.

Yet is this our experience? Sometimes the battle leaves us quite wounded. Where are the angels then? There are few things to mention

6. Keener, *Revelation*, 321; Wall, *Revelation*, 162.

7. Morris, *Revelation*, 160.

here. First is that we do not know how bad things could have been if the angels had not battled on our behalf. We only see one part of the story, probably the more painful part, and this can color our view. Yet this is natural—our pain informs our attitudes. This is human, but we should nonetheless raise our eyes and give thanks that things could always have been much worse. Second, and linked to this, is that well-known story of the footsteps on the beach of life, and for much of life there are two sets of footprints—ours and God's. The complaint comes though that in the bad times of life, there is only one set of footprints—I walked alone. But, said God, that this was "when I carried you." Similarly, sometimes angels have walked with us, and we have not known it.

What these both say is that we do not always see the help. Dan 10 is a good story which helps us in these situations. He had been praying and fasting for three weeks, and then he was given a vision. The vision was so tangible and real that those around him, who could not see it, nevertheless sensed the presence and ran to hide. The fiery figure loved, blessed, and affirmed Daniel before saying to him: "Fear not, Daniel, for from the first day that you set your heart to understand and humbled yourself before your God, your words have been heard, and I have come because of your words. The prince of the kingdom of Persia withstood me twenty-one days, but Michael, one of the chief princes, came to help me, for I was left there with the kings of Persia, and came to make you understand what is to happen to your people in the latter days." (Dan 10:12–14)

As soon as Daniel started to pray and fasted for answers, wisdom, and understanding, heaven heard the prayer and responded. However, Daniel only got the vision *three weeks later*. The prayer, in human terms, wasn't answered instantly. In heavenly terms, the response was immediate. The delay was caused by a battle between the fiery figure and the prince of Persia, and a resolution only came when Michael came to support the fiery figure. It took a battle and it took time for the answer to come.

Quite what this passage exactly means is unclear, and commentators have widely varying opinions on the matter, as well as the precise identity of the fiery figure. Presumably he is an angel (angels could have the appearance of lightning, Matt 28:3), who then enlisted further angelic help on his difficult mission. This battle echoes the angelic fighting of Rev 12, which required war to be waged. Angels fighting angels means there is no easy push over, even though the final result is always known. The Lamb wins!

Nevertheless, the point stands, that prayer is heard instantly, heaven responds instantly, but it can take time for that to be visibly shown in our lives on earth. Prayer may not be immediately answered by angelic ministers but this delay should not be interpreted as a lack of action on God's part, or the part of his angels. Sometimes waiting for an answer we experience a delay, yet, and this is worth remembering, the fiery figure and Michael won the day and the answer arrived, eventually.

ANGELS, HEALING, AND HEAVEN

Two final points need to be made, which further enrich what it means to be healed, and how angels are a part of that process. First, one must mention worship. Fully discussed later, it is worth knowing that worship is much more than singing to God. It is an activity that brings communion with God and transports us into his presence. And in his presence, is healing. Worship is the principal act by which we are changed ever more into what God calls us to be—his image. It is a life-shaping and life-changing act: "Worship is a door open in heaven. We lift up our hearts, listen to what God is saying, join the angels and archangels and all the saints in heaven in praising God's eternal holiness. Worship is a door open to the inner depths of life . . . Worship is a door open to the rhythms of life . . . Worship is a door to our hearts open in obedience to God . . . And as we worship we are changed."[8]

As we worship, we are changed. We are transformed steadily into his image and likeness, where our marring by sin is rubbed away, and the true image given by God, holy, healed and whole, shines through. God, through his angelic ministers, heals, and removes obstacles that people may face in life, and this freedom becomes a spur to worship, praise and serve God with even more vigor. But further still, and ancient and modern liturgies overflow with this truth, angels are themselves leading and inspiring us to, and in, worship, taking us to meet with God. "Therefore with Angels and Archangels, and with all the company of heaven, we laude and magnify Thy glorious name, evermore, praising Thee, and

---

8. *New Patterns for Worship*, 26–27; cf. Bradshaw (ed.), *Companion to Common Worship II*, 108–20.

saying: 'Holy, Holy, Holy, Lord God of Hosts, heaven and earth are full of your glory.'"

The worship given by the angels in heaven is awesome to consider, and it is here in heaven we see the last part of the healing journey, and at the very end, angels remain at our sides, taking us to glory.

The glorious life of heaven is often in our sights, but also often strangely absent too, especially in the midst of trial and suffering and seemingly unanswered prayer. Sometimes we do not see or experience a fullness of healing here on earth, and so our eyes need to turn and look toward heaven for the completion of the process. Through this, angels can help to paint a picture of the full and ultimate healing that we will find in heaven. We can be assured that our souls will be taken to heaven. Luke 16:22–23 gives comfort to those facing death: "The poor man died and was carried by the angels to Abraham's side. The rich man also died and was buried, and in Hades, being in torment, he lifted up his eyes and saw Abraham far off and Lazarus at his side."

Lazarus was carried by the angels to the heavenly feast, to eat at Abraham's side. Leaving aside the honor of being a guest at that blessed table, angels took Lazarus there, in a heavenly and angelic cortège, and made sure he would not miss out on what God had promised for him. Compare this with the simple bleak summary for the rich man, who *died and was buried*. This is comfort, and many funeral liturgies use this idea to console those mourning. Anglican Funeral Prayers echo the idea of angels carrying Poor Lazarus. The soul is comforted with assurance of being heaven bound: "Go forth on your journey from this world . . . aided by angels, archangels and all the armies of the heavenly host . . . and bring us at last to the wholeness and fullness of your presence."[9]

Angels will carry our souls to the heavenly society, with the angels. In heaven there will be no more pain or tears, and Rev 12 says there is no place for dragons/demons in heaven. We will rest in a place without evil, or the threat of evil; a place with only joy and worship, and a welcome to feast in a community transformed by God's grace.

"Aided by the angels . . . may your portion be in peace today and your dwelling in the heavenly Jerusalem."[10]

This new home will be accompanied by a new body—a resurrection body—and as we have already seen from Luke 20:36 this will be like, or

9. *Common Worship (Pastoral Services)*, 229; cf. 255, 376.

10. Ibid., 229.

equal to, the angels. What does this enigmatic phrase mean? Well, Jesus, unhelpfully, doesn't tell us, but actually assumes that his hearers know exactly what he is talking about! Commentators have come up with various options. Clearly it is linked with the gift of immortality that the resurrection affords us, but it also resonates elsewhere. John Nolland says that the word "*like the angels*" (*isangelloi* / ισαγγελοι), which is unique to Luke, speaks of "a certain kind of heavenly glory and dignity of form, that comes with it freedom from demise through bodily decline, disease or accident."[11] Nolland rightly highlights that it is something more than a change of status, but includes somehow possessing some of the qualities of the angels, and from his quote we see that it must be the result of some kind of healing/wholeness process which can never be overturned or reversed. However, it not nature alone that it speaks of, but, as Morris pinpoints, it is also a statement of a place within the heavenly society with other sons of God, since it means being "taken up into the fullness of life in the family of God."[12] This also then speaks of a healing of relationships, with God and with the wider family of God (saints and angels). The healing is more than just about our nature, but is also of our characters and lives, and thus our ability to relate to others.

At this point I should dispel any thoughts that *being like the angels* means we will become ghostly beings in the ether wandering the earth, or chubby cherubs with wings. What this phrase points to is the absolute fullness of a totally healed and whole, sin-free human body—like the body Jesus had after his resurrection. This body was one which could both eat and be touched, and yet could walk through walls, appear almost out-of-nowhere, and not be instantly recognised—some interesting parallels to the bodies that angels seem to have when on earth. N. T. Wright's book *Surprised by Hope* spells out the physicality of the New Heaven and New Earth. To be sure it is a new and fully-redeemed physicality of which we have no current experience, but physical it is.[13] The near unanimous orthodox verdict of the past 2000 years is that angels have bodies of a kind, but we do not know what that body is, other than it is spiritual, but can take on physical form when required.[14] Angels too

11. Nolland, *Luke*, 966. N. T. Wright finds a few echoes in other ancient literature, while recognising the word's basic rarity. Wright, *Resurrection of the Son of God*, 423.

12. Morris, *Luke*, 319.

13. Wright, *Surprised by Hope*.

14. The fact that Satan can be tormented in fire (Rev 20:10) indicates that he (as an

have the propensity to fall (as the demons demonstrate), and despite being "holy," Scripture tells us that God can still charge them with folly (Job 4:18). However, angels are now confirmed and perfected by God's grace, and by nothing of their own, and in this grace-filled state cannot fall. Yet remove God's grace, and they would be as likely to fall as we do.[15] Angels then are not so far removed from us: perilously close to falling, yet by God's grace a million miles away from doing so. This too is what it is *to be like unto the angels*, and Jesus' resurrection body and his appearances also give a glimpse into what it will mean for us.

Yet in the face of personal suffering, one can doubt that God can heal like this. It is hard enough to accept that in this fallen world in our hurting bodies we are said, even now, to be "a little lower than the angels" (Ps 8:5–6 LXX: Lit. "heavenly beings"). How often do you feel as if you are a little lower than the angels? It is hard enough knowing who we now are, let alone see what we will be. If we do not see the power of God in the present, maybe we begin to doubt that he has that power. How do we know that we will be fully healed? What is the evidence and proof that God gives that he can transform us? Pastorally, we need to be able to give confidence that God can, does and will do these amazing things, and there are two ways to do this, again showing how pastoral angelology cannot be held in isolation from other parts of theology. First is the resurrection of Christ, which is *the* one proof that death does not and cannot prevail over created beings. The second is that God can take a created being and make it immortal, sinless, worshipful, and joyful, living in an evil-free zone. Angels show what God can do to a created nature. Since we are told that we, in our resurrected bodies, will be *like unto the angels*, then looking at the angels will start to show what fullness of healing and fullness of Life is, and by this we can have confidence that God will complete the good work begun in us. *Isangelloi* means that God will give us not only healed and whole bodies, but also healed and whole relationships with himself and everybody else in heaven. It points to a total restoration of every aspect of ourselves and our lives, and this is a truth we can encourage people with.

---

angelic being) has a body of some kind which can be punished, like the beast and the false prophet, who are with him.

15. Macy, *Angels (1547–1662)*, ch. 3.

The whole Christian life is a journey of healing on numerous levels—physical, emotional and spiritual—all with the aim of bringing us closer to God and his will. Angels help us on our way along the road and they model what a healed life looks like both now, and how it will ultimately be in heaven. Angels are a gift from God to prove that what he did in Christ works for all created beings, and the perfection of the angels is the perfection we too will enjoy.

However, journeys are rarely short affairs, especially the journey of life. On that journey we will need sustaining, and the strength to face both good times and bad. Paul exhorts us to run the race to the end, and not stop half-way. However, too often it is a common pattern of life to run out of steam and energy, and then give up. And God's angels know this and part of their ministry is to help us in this weakness. So how can angels provide us with spiritual and physical sustenance on our journey?

6

ANGELS AND SUSTAINING

Once healing has begun and the journey started, you need to be sure that you will have the resources to complete it. You will need to be sustained. The ministry of sustaining has four aspects to it. First, it *preserves* the situation with as little loss as possible, aiming to hold the line against other threats, further loss, or excessive retreat.[1] Second, it offers *consolation* that the loss incurred does not negate one's destiny in God, and that one is not alone in the midst of the suffering. It is relief from misery, acknowledging the negative experience, while not providing a solution.[2] It is the shoulder to cry on, or the encouraging word to keep going, but not the answer to the problem. Third is *consolidation*, so that one can build a platform from which to then face life. Resources are marshalled to face the future, and any loss is seen as a partial not total loss, so hope remains and can be built upon.[3] It is the renewal of right perspective. Fourth is *redemption* which is found by facing, then embracing, the loss in order to set out again to achieve God's destiny.[4] It is the journey to *begin to build an on-going life that once more pursues its fulfilment and destiny on a new basis.*[5]

PRAYER

Before embarking on the specifics of angels and the ministry of sustaining, I want to tackle the area of angels and prayer, since prayer is not only an activity which sustains us all, but is one which underpins all pastoral care. In the same way that worship is more than singing, so prayer is

1. Clebsch and Jaekle *Pastoral*, 44.
2. Ibid., 47.
3. Ibid., 47.
4. Ibid., 43.
5. Ibid., 48.

more than simply speaking with God. And in the same way that worship can cross many pastoral boundaries, so can aspects of prayer.

However, prayer is here in the chapter on sustaining, because it is the pastoral activity of being with a person in need who struggles to stand alone, who needs support and sustaining. We all know how, when we are worried, struggling, or in dire straits, our spirits can be lifted when somebody prays for us, and even more so when we know that our church is also praying for us—what a comfort and blessing! In this context praying is incredibly powerful and encouraging. Prayer assists in all aspects of sustaining, since prayer can be aimed at any part of the pastoral process. That angels pray and intercede for us undergirds the whole process.

That we should pray and petition God is not in question. It is also not in question that we should ask friends and fellow Christians to pray for us. Neither is it in question that when we do ask people to pray for us, and they do, it is a good, powerful, and effective thing. The question is, why do we need angels to pray with and for us?

For most of us, prayer is hard work and does not come naturally. And even for those of us who can pray easily, we wonder if we are praying rightly. Are we really in tune with the Holy Spirit and the will of God? Whereas we may grow weary of prayer, and may not know what to pray, angels who see us and stand in the heavenly council, know exactly what to petition God for. Their prayer is always well informed, and they never weary of praying. There is one God and one mediator, Jesus Christ, but as there are many humans on earth who pray and intercede, so too are there angels who do exactly the same.

The book of Revelation regularly uses the image of prayer as incense, and it is here that we see how angels and prayer interrelate. Rev 8 paints a beautiful picture of this: "And another angel came and stood at the altar with a golden censer, and he was given much incense to offer with the prayers of all the saints on the golden altar before the throne, and the smoke of the incense, with the prayers of the saints, rose before God from the hand of the angel" (Rev 8:3–4).

Some commentators make no comment on the relationship between angels and prayer. Others betray their theological backgrounds, dismissing it as a nice but ultimately meaningless image, or alternatively bury it in endless comments about there only being one mediator, and that we should not worship angels. However, some theologians do try and take seriously what it says and what it implies. The angel is said to have his own incense (prayers), and a lot of it too, which is offered *with* the prayers of the saints, and before the altar they are presented together, as one, to God by the angel. Morris writes: "Notice (the prayers) went up out of the angel's hand. This is probably a way of saying that heaven and earth are one in the matter. Prayer is not the lonely venture it so often feels. There is heavenly assistance and our prayers do reach God."[6]

Angels are involved in prayer with humans and presenting our prayers to God, their assistance being both in the presentation of human prayers as well as adding to our prayers with their own, but a further interesting aspect is shown in Job 33. Elihaz—the only one of Job's friends not condemned by God—is listing ways that God speaks to humans, to guide them, and especially to correct them. God communicates in many ways, in dreams, opening ears for his voice, and through chastening pain (Job 33:14–19). Then he says: "If there be for him an angel, a mediator, one of the thousand, to declare to man what is right for him, and he is merciful to him, and says, 'Deliver him from going down into the pit; I have found a ransom; let his flesh become fresh with youth; let him return to the days of his youthful vigour'; Then [the] man prays to God, and he accepts him; he sees his face with a shout of joy, and he restores to (the) man his righteousness" (Job 33:23–26).

Here an angel is referred to as a mediator, one who stands alongside, who tells somebody what is right and mercifully asks God not to condemn them but to renew and heal them. This then leads the person him/herself (v. 26) to pray and find acceptance, joy, and righteousness from God. The angel intercedes, God hears this, and the outcome is the renewal of the individual's prayer life and walk with God. The outcome is not the individual's reliance on angelic prayer but the revitalization of his/her own spiritual life. Clines sums it up neatly: "It only needs a word on the sufferer's behalf by one of the many intercessory angels and the person is healed and offers public thanksgiving for restoration to health. That person then makes a confession of sin."[7]

There is a power in angelic intercession and prayer, which can lead to somebody's life being substantially changed, renewed and reinvigorated. Angels see the face of God, and they are not silent when in that position, but advocate on the behalf of their charges. The context of

6. Morris, *Revelation*, 121.

7. Clines, *Job*, 479.

Matt 18:10 is children, but their prayer is not limited to children—one only needs to consider Gabriel's coming in response to Daniel's prayer. While children are a specially highlighted case, all Christians share this blessing and privilege of angelic intercession over their lives. Angels are "watchers" (Dan 4:13) who observe events on earth, and so know what to pray. We have already read in Jas 5:16 that the prayers of a righteous man are powerful and effective. How much more so the holy angels on God's council who see God's face?

Angels come in response to prayers of the faithful. We see it in Dan 10, and while there was a delay, Daniel was told that as soon as he prayed, it was heard in heaven and the answer was set in motion to come to him. Similarly, we see it in Acts 12, where Peter is in prison. The believers pray for his release and an angel comes and does as they requested, and they were so surprised at the answer (probably because they did the same for James, but with no apparent success) they did not believe it at first!

The work of angels praying for us is something to not only thank God for, but also to inspire us in our prayer lives. If angelic prayer can have the life-changing impact that we see in Job 33, surely we should be petitioning God and expecting the same. However, one should never say that the angelic assistance in prayer and intercession is a substitute for our own prayer life. Prayer is the primary way that we have relationship with God, and this is something angels can never do on our behalf. We are called into relationship with God directly. The angels' prayer supports us. It is a support not an alternative. Just as a human prayer partner can only support one's Christian life and not live it for you, so angels can only support what we already have and do, and cannot replace or be an alternative to our life with and in Christ. As with Christ in Gethsemane, the angel came to strengthen him so he could carry on his conversation with God. The angel did not tell Jesus to take a rest while he took over. Christ prayed and always prayed. The angel simply strengthened him to carry on.

Do we pray to angels, or ask angels to pray for us? Orthodox and Catholic traditions would take the parallel with human intercessors and say that since we can ask them, we can ask angels as well. However, while I understand the line of logic, I feel very uncomfortable taking that extra step. For while there are many biblical examples of people asking for others to pray for them, there is not one example of a human praying to an angel. Scripture does not take that extra step, nor does it seem to invite us too either. And, when considering the example of Jesus, we see he never asked for the help of angels, but nonetheless received it as a gift from the Father. I therefore believe we should feel content that angels watch us, know us, and know the face of God. Angels know exactly what to pray about regarding our situations. They do not need us to ask them anything for they know better than ourselves what to pray.

PRESERVATION

In order to preserve a situation, one needs to protect what is there. The area of angelic protection is rich, and we have already looked at how angels protect us from demonic assault, and other problems in life. Angels journey with people, protect them from threat and evil, pray for people, counsel people away from wrong decisions, lead people into healing, help them to pray, praise and focus upon God. As the Anglican liturgy says, angels *help (succour) and defend us on earth.*[8] We are assured that we will not hurt our feet (Ps 91), and that the angel of the Lord encamps around those who fear him and rescues them (Ps 34). Nevertheless, despite these wonderful promises, one should be careful not to preach or teach an over-optimistic and victorious theology, where one will never face struggle or discord. Simply looking at our lives and the lives of those around us, should teach the reality of the battle; the now-but-not-yet. Both Dan 10 and Rev 12 show that although victory is assured, it is not without battle and struggle, or some delay in final answers coming.

The idea of protection allows us also to consider the question of guardian angels. It is striking how often, when talking about angels, I have found that the conversation comes around to whether or not we have our own guardian angel. It is a question which intrigues and confuses, attracts and repels. One might call it the sharp end of angelology, the point where everything can either come into glorious focus and light, or be plunged into ever more distant spirals of alienation. For if guardian angels do exist then one would need to develop a level of richness in one's angelology to do justice to the concept. God would not give us guardian angels, if they, in the final analysis, didn't do anything. Yet, if they do not exist, there is no need for development or any deep understanding of angels, since every form of guardianship can come under the direct action of God, bypassing any need for angels.

---

8. *Common Worship*, 441, 514 (Michaelmas Collect).

Where does the biblical justification for guardian angels come from? There are a number of verses which are used to demonstrate the idea. For example: "This poor man cried, and the Lord heard him and saved him out of all his troubles. The angel of the Lord encamps around those who fear him, and delivers them" (Ps 34:6–7). "For he will command his angels concerning you, to guard you in all your ways" (Ps 91:11).

Ps 34 says that, in response to a cry to God, that an angel encamps around the God-fearing. Angels set up camp around us, which is a more permanent idea than a flitting in and out of our lives occasionally. And, since camps are able to be picked up and moved as the scene of action moves, as we move, so the angels follow. Note, though, that in Ps 34 that the word "angel" is singular, whilst in Ps 91 it is plural: Angels seem to work both alone and in teams. But to do what? Guard us in all our ways. Not some of our ways sometimes, but *all* our ways.

Angels guard us, and this book bears testimony to that on-going truth. Many see this as a generalised protection, but the passages above appear to narrow it down to individuals. God sends an individual angel to an individual person to help them. The question then arises, is it the same angel that comes each time, or is there some kind of rotational system where the nearest or best-equipped one goes, so a different angel comes each time? A few verses may suggest that there is a rotational system or a zone defence (as Wayne Grudem puts it), but it seems not to be the exclusive answer to the question.[9]

First, we read in Matt 18:10: "See that you do not despise one of these little ones. For I tell you that in heaven their angels always see the face of my Father who is in heaven." The phrase *"their* angels" points, in the Greek, to the idea that each one of the children has their own angel, and this is not an angelic team effort to protect a group of children. It is individualised and singular and each angel stands before God on behalf of the child. To see God's face is not the passive act of merely observing him, but, as with the imagery of the angelic council, it involves speaking, pleading, and praying. This angelic ministry is active, individualised and right in the throne room of heaven.

In Acts 12, we read that Peter was released from jail by an angel and led through the town by this same angel to the place where the disciples and others were praying. Rhoda the servant girl opened the door to him, and, overcome with joy, she left Peter locked outside and went

9. Grudem, *Systematic Theology*, 399–400.

to the meeting to tell them. There was disbelief in the group, and we read: "They said to her, 'You are out of your mind.' But she kept insisting that it was so, and they kept saying, 'It is his angel!'"(Acts 12:15: ESV). Literally, "*the angel, it is, of him*"—it is Peter's angel. Belief in guardian angels was common in Jewish thought and theology, and the idea that the angel looked like their charge was also emerging at that time too.[10] This statement suggests that the apostles and disciples in the room believed Peter had his own angel. Some scholars say the comment was a sarcastic sideswipe at a lowly servant girl, and so can be discounted. But the wider context doesn't sit easily with this view. At first they ridiculed her, but her continued insistence, confidence, and total assurance made them change their tack. Clearly Rhoda had seen something/someone who looked like Peter. Their derision (the derision, note, of a group of apostles and disciples against one girl) did not change her mind, and her staunch insistence meant they needed to change their response and somehow explain it. In doing so they arrived at the common Jewish idea that it was Peter's (guardian) angel. This was the only explanation which made sense.[11]

These individualised or specialised ministries are echoed elsewhere. Dan 10:2–21 (cf. 12:1) speaks of angels overseeing nations, but not necessarily only good angels. There is a prince—an angel—of Israel (Michael), but another of Greece and one of Persia. Areas can have their own angel. Similarly, the churches in Rev 1–3 are said to have their own angels.[12] And all this leads back to Heb 1:14, and the exposition of chapter 1.

While it is true that none of these verses provide the single knock-out punch as proof for guardian angels, they clearly focus the angelic ministry very personally and individually, and taking the next step is not doing any discernable damage to the texts or contexts. Guardian angels are never excluded as a possibility, but in fact, if anything, the evidence

10. The first mention of this idea seems to have been Acts 12:15, with no other explicit contemporary evidence for the idea of the guardian angel looking like their charge, but it appears in slightly later Jewish thought, and similarly has echoes in some early Christian literature (e.g., Herm. *Vis.* 5:7). Marshall *Acts*, 210; cf. Stack and Billerbeck, *Kommentaur* II, 707.

11. Some translations miss this subtlety. However, many make clear that the insistent position of Rhoda led to change of approach by those in the meeting. A good reading of the passage would be: "'You're out of your mind,' they said to her. But she kept telling them it was true. So they said, 'It must be his angel'" (NIRV).

12. Rev 2:1, 8, 12, 18; 3:1, 7, 14.

is placed upon the table for serious consideration, which points to the possibility they are real.

My personal opinion is that it is far more likely than not that we have a guardian angel. I also believe that angels can work together in a "zone-defence," but this is in addition to the personalised guardian angel. I recognise that the Bible is not clear in this, and there is enough lack of clarity for caution to be expressed. However, if one takes the passages which point that way, and hold that with the richness of the biblical witness to angelic ministry in general, one must ask, why have such a rich ministry if it is, effectively, not used for the benefit of individual believers? Add to this the huge weight of history where the majority of theologians and Christians during most of Christian history have believed in them, and I must confess that I would not bet on there not being guardian angels. I would not be surprised if, when we get to glory, we find we have one with a whole host of stories about how they were invisibly enriching our lives by their work. Therefore, unless one has a wider theology which, for preconceived reasons, precludes the possibility, I think guardian angels are the most reasonable understanding to what these texts suggest.

Angels protect and thus preserve us, but if this is so, why do we still have problems, pain and accidents? The angels don't seem to be doing a good job! The answer to this, on many levels, parallels the wider question over God's goodness if there is pain in the world. To be comfortable with God's good providence amid a troubled and violent world, allows one to be comfortable with angelic protection in the same context. Angels do protect and preserve, yet one difficult aspect of this, from the point of view of humanity, is that we rarely see them at work. If you consider Daniel in the Lion's Den (Dan 6), King Nebuchadnezzar spent a whole night deeply troubled, desperately hoping and praying for Daniel's safety (Dan 6:18). So while, in the morning, the king was overjoyed that his prayers had been answered by angels holding the lion's mouths closed (6:22), this was only *after* his night of anguish. Angels work invisibly and there can be a time-lapse before we see or know what they have done for us.

CONSOLATION

When we are in a difficult situation, more than anything else we need to know we are not alone, or abandoned. We need *consolation* that these troubled times do not negate our destiny in God, and that we are not alone in the midst of the suffering. Consolation is also the shoulder to cry on, the encouraging word to keep going, but not the answer to the problem. Consolation can be shown in two, not mutually exclusive, ways. First is the truth that help and assistance is on the way. Second is the personal touch, the loving presence, the actual physical shoulder provided for crying upon. Head and heart are engaged together to console.

As we have already seen, in Dan 10 the fiery figure came in answer to Daniel's prayer, but there was a delay—a delay made shorter by the intervention of archangel Michael. Prayer will be answered, and the angels will ensure this is so, but maybe not instantaneously and the situation may last longer than one wishes. However, the answer comes and the destiny is not overturned by the delay. Similarly, in Rev 12, there is a battle in heaven, where Satan fought back. Satan loses and is ejected, but now down on earth continues the fight. Michael's victory took time, but finally the demons were expelled (12:7), so comprehensively that there was no place for them to return. Victory is assured and coming, but in the final skirmishes with the evil one, people still get hurt.

Personally, I am often inspired by the story in 2 Kgs 6:8–17, which says to me that though we may not see the help that God sends, and though we may be deeply frightened by the situation we are facing, the (victorious) heavenly host is surrounding us, though we do not see it. Israel was protected, and the enemy soldiers were struck blind the next day. The expected rout did not happen, and the story ends with the soldiers being taken to the king, and treated as guests not enemies. Good relationship was restored between the nations. Yet, note, the angels did not have to destroy the enemy army to return the land to peace. Angels are sent by God to resolve situations, and they do so, but not necessarily how we might expect!

And this continues after Pentecost: in Acts 12 we read of an angel freeing Peter from jail. Here is a story of persecution and incarceration for the faith, instigated by an evil ruler intent on murderous ways—as his killing of James plainly testifies. There was no divine intervention for James. Peter must have been terrified, wondering what would come next: is he going to go the same way as James? However, an angel came in response to prayer, freed Peter from jail, and protected him from re-arrest as he escaped. Not only that, by the end of the chapter, God had also dealt with Herod by sending an angel to kill him.

These are some of the passages which we could use as proof that God's angelic cavalry is coming over the hill to save the day, and so provide comfort. Yet we humans, as beings of flesh, bone, and emotion, also need more physical and tangible support.

With that in mind, let's reflect upon the words spoken to Mary by the angel in Luke 1:28: "Greetings, O favoured one, the Lord is with you!" We see a warm welcome, a statement of who Mary is to reassure her that this is not a negative visit of judgement, and an assurance of God's presence. It is a beautifully crafted opening statement designed to reduce Mary's anxiety and fear, and allow her to hear the life changing news that is coming her way. Gabriel later calls Mary by name (v. 30), a personal and intimate act that further decreases the tension and stress of the encounter.

Similarly we could think about how the angels at the tomb of Jesus, when faced with the distraught women, gently and lovingly helped them through the confusion and trauma to go and tell people what had happened. Mary Magdalene's instinct, when she got the chance, was to stay at Jesus' feet, but the angel guided her away from him, and toward proclaiming the resurrection. It is worth pondering here why God sent an angel to do this. Why have an intermediary, for the want of a better word? Why couldn't Jesus have met them himself, as he later did? There is no obvious answer, but clearly it was God's good pleasure to have, prior to Jesus' appearance, an angel announce the resurrection and introduce the idea to the women and disciples before they were faced with the real thing. For all the awesome presence an angel brings, it seems to have been the better first option, than Jesus himself. It feels as if there was some preparation going on. It was an easier way in to introduce the incredible new reality. God first used the angel, which in itself would have indicated to the people that God was present and active specifically in that place. The angel's presence said *"Something has happened here. Look and listen carefully!"* This then paved the way for the women and disciples to encounter the greater event, and meet the resurrected Jesus. Almost like an extra step in raising their eyes, the angel was consoling, teaching, and then commissioning, readying them for the greater and more amazing truth that was to be revealed.

CONSOLIDATION

Consolidation allows one to build a platform from which to face life. Any loss is placed in a wider context, and remaining hope is built upon. It is the renewal of right perspective, and the platform from which one can re-launch or rebuild the godly life.

One could say that simply the on-going knowledge and assurance of God's love and protection, shown through his angels, is a good plank which could be used in the foundation. Angels are always there support-ing us through life. As one Anglican prayer says: "[Angels] keep a faithful vigil for us, guarding us along the way that leads to life, and guiding us towards the kingdom of your light."[13]

However it is not enough. In 1 Cor 3, the foundation is said to be Jesus Christ, and any pastoral solution must, at some point, direct people to him. What is built on Christ is the temple of the Holy Spirit, the temple of God, and this individual temple is but one brick in a bigger temple. We have already noted how post-Pentecost angelic ministry always points one to Christ and his gospel, but once someone is a Christian, what then? Life does not end, and in fact it has only just begun. How do we build, and what do we build? It is the holy, obedient life that is pleasing to God. Angels, as we shall see, are not only protectors, but also *exemplars* of how to serve God, and they can help us build a life that is pleasing to God. The holy angels model the godly life.

Simply to apply the prefix "holy" speaks of how angels live. This term appears in the Old Testament, and so this is the context for holy to apply to angels. "Holy" implies both separation and differentiation from the normal, common, or profane. God, as the Holy One, is therefore distinct and sacred—set apart as one of a unique kind—and therefore he alone is worthy of praise and worship. "Holy" can be equivalent to "Godhead" or simply "divine" (Dan 4:8, 9, 18; 5:11), but can also describe God's at-tributes, like his arm (Isa 52:10; Ps 98:1) or Name (Lev 20:3). God is the *Holy One*, *Holy God*, and the *Holy One of Israel*.[14] Therefore, the term "holy" is not one thrown around lightly. With this in mind, the fact that angels are called "holy ones" is not a casual aside, or loose prefix.[15] It says something of their nature, and so their role too.

---

13. *Common Worship (Festivals)*, 113.

14. Isa 40:25; 1 Sam 6:20; 2 Kgs 19:22; Ps 71:22; Isa 5:16; 41:14; Jer 50:29; Hab 1:12.

15. Deut 33:2–3; Job 5:1; 15:15; Ps 89:5, 7; Dan 4:17; Zech 14:5.

The contrast with this prefix for humans is important. First, in the Old Testament "holy" is, unlike the angels, rarely linked with humans, although in the New Testament, as temples of the Holy Spirit, Christians are called saints, or "hagioi" (literally "holy ones"; e.g., Eph 1:15, Heb 3:1; Rev 18:20). Yet, when it is used in the Old Testament, for example where Israel will be the holy people of God, the driving use of the word is that they "will" or "shall" be holy, but were not fully so at that time. While personal holiness is something humans can know something of now, its permanent fullness is a future state. Thus some texts allude to a present aspect, but that seems more like God's declaration of separation in the present which will lead to the future state, as opposed to the idea of completeness in the here and now.[16] After the events of the Exodus, one could never say the Israelites were holy, but they were still set apart as God's special people, called to live holy lives, who would become, in time, that holy people as God envisaged.[17]

The only other time "holy" is applied to people is in Dan 8:24 and 12:7. However this again has a future and eschatological aspect to it, being applied to people in a vision of the future. Individual humans are never called "holy"—in a moral sense—in the here and now. Angels, however, *are* called holy, and this too points to what it will be *to be like the angels*. The angelic state gives us a picture of what we will be like in glory. Therefore, we can look with confidence at the life and work of the angels, and then look to emulate what they do. We can be imitators of them, just as Paul in 1 Cor 11:1 calls upon the church to imitate him, as he imitated Christ. Angels imitate and model the holy life of the Triune God, Father, Son, and Holy Spirit. We should not be afraid to imitate them.

For example, Ps 103 tells of angels who do his bidding and obey his word, and, alongside praise and worship, this is expressed in the huge range of tasks that characterise angelic ministry—*those sent to serve those who will inherit salvation*. Our obedience must not only be an inwardly turned holiness, but also outwardly turned to express this to our neighbours. Angels are before God praying, serving, working, worshipping and blessing—this whole book is testimony to the witness

16. Exod 19:6; Deut 26:19; 28:9; cf. 14:2, 21; Isa 62:12; cf. 63:18; cf. Durham *Exodus*, 263; cf. Noth, *Exodus*, 157.

17. Isa 62:12; cf. Young *Isaiah*, 473.

angels give us of the godly outwardly turned holiness which blesses the rest of creation.

We are to love God and our neighbours as ourselves, and the biblical stories of angelic ministry show us how we may do this. We could do much worse than imitate the angels' concern for the welfare of God's creation and people.

For humans, obedience is achieved by obeying Holy Spirit. It would unfair, then, if we had to be obedient in a way other than the angels. If the angels can be obedient without the Holy Spirit, what can that teach us? However, angels provide us with an incredible challenge and model to aspire to, because it is by the Spirit they live and work. Ezek 1 speaks of an incredible vision that the prophet had, and this vision was filled, through and through, by the Spirit of God:

> And each went straight forward. Wherever the spirit would go, they went, without turning as they went . . . And the living creatures darted to and fro, like the appearance of a flash of lightning. Now as I looked at the living creatures, I saw a wheel on the earth beside the living creatures, one for each of the four of them . . . And when the living creatures went, the wheels went beside them; and when the living creatures rose from the earth, the wheels rose. Wherever the spirit wanted to go, they went, and the wheels rose along with them, for the spirit of the living creatures was in the wheels. When those went, these went; and when those stood, these stood; and when those rose from the earth, the wheels rose along with them, for the spirit of the living creatures was in the wheels. (Ezek 1:12, 14–15, 19–21)

There is some debate as to what "spirit" means here. Eichrodt nails his colors to the mast and says: "For the prophet himself, the power [the heavenly beings used] to move is derived solely from the mighty Spirit . . . [The heavenly beings] are ruled by the might of the Spirit streaming through them."[18]

For some there is an unwillingness to say that it is the Spirit of God that Ezekiel has in mind. Some ignore the idea completely, and speak of wind, modern physics, and propellers.[19] However, this is rare, and most recognise the spirit is a force of God, and so call it the vital energy or

---

18. Eichrodt, *Ezekiel*, 57.

19. Brownlee, *Ezekiel*, 13.

impulse God used to direct the heavenly beings,[20] or the life-giving, energizing power of God,[21] or the manifestation of God's omnipresence.[22] Quite what the difference between these three ideas and the indwelling and directing of Holy Spirit himself is not clear, yet the reluctance to make the direct link that Eichrodt makes, is obvious. Wright, however, like Eichrodt, makes clear the full implications of the passage: "The whole dynamic scene, even before Ezekiel has been able to take it all in, is animated by the spirit that he recognised as the Spirit of the living God—the same Spirit that would be needed to revive and empower the prophet himself (2:2; 3:24)."[23]

What empowered Ezekiel and gave him life was what empowered the heavenly beings—the Holy Spirit—and the angels were obedient to the Spirit. Where the Spirit went, the angels went without turning. Wherever the Spirit wanted to go, the angels followed, and the description throughout Ezekiel's vision is of straight lines, with no wandering or deviation. Pure and unswerving obedience to the prompting and direction of the Spirit.

At this point, we maybe begin to resolve why the work of the Holy Spirit can look similar to the work of angels. Angels, as holy heavenly beings, full of the Spirit and with no sin to taint this, operate in exact conformity to the Spirit. Angels are holy spirits who perfectly obey the Holy Spirit. It is therefore no surprise that in doing the will of the Spirit perfectly, their work looks like what the Spirit would want and do. Just as when we do what Jesus wants, we show something of the image of Christ, so when angels perfectly do the will of the Spirit, they can look like the Spirit.

Secondly, as we saw earlier in the book, angels observe our lives, which should be an encouragement to live godly lives. As we live our lives, we are on a stage before the angels (and if we have a guardian angel, this is more poignant). It requires us to be aware of how we should live and act. As we have seen, Paul demands proper order in church *because of the angels*,[24] and the principle of rebuking sinners so that others will

---

20. Taylor, *Ezekiel*, 56.

21. Block, *Ezekiel*, 101.

22. Allen, *Ezekiel*, 32.

23. Wright, *Ezekiel*, 50.

24. As noted in ch. 1, some Jews thought, on the basis of Gen 6, that fallen angelic beings saw the beauty of human women, took them, and procreated with them to pro-

be fearful of doing wrong, which is undergirded by knowing one is before the angels (1 Tim 5:21). This idea of a stage is also found in Matt 18:10 and the heavenly council who, while having earthly charges, see God's face, and because of this, we are told "see that you do not despise these little ones". Other examples would be, for example, 1 Cor 4:9: "For I think that God has exhibited us apostles as last of all, like men sentenced to death, because we have become a spectacle to the world, to angels, and to men." There is a barb behind Paul's comment here, but the force is clear. *Everything* we do in God's service, including motives and actions, is on display to heaven as well as earth, so reflect on how you minister and what and who you think you are.

These verses find their force not simply in the idea of being on a stage before such awesome beings, but that the beings are holy, standing before God, and charged with ensuring our safety, and guarding us in all our ways. If angels had no mission to us and did not care, these passages would have little resonance or force. The verses have power because of the intimate mission of angels toward us. The presence of the angels alongside Christ (the Son) and God (the Father) means that their presence around us too, is to be taken seriously as we live our lives. We are to behave in an obedient and godly manner because we are before other created beings who live in an obediently and godly manner. We know Heb 13:1–2: "Keep on loving each other as brothers. Do not forget to entertain strangers, for by so doing some people have entertained angels without knowing it." We are called to give hospitality and love for our brethren, not only because they are good things to do, but also because one may actually be faced with an angel of God. And this warning that we will one day face an angel of God, should also ensure we have right judgement and forgiving hearts:

> When one of you has a grievance against another, does he dare go to law before the unrighteous instead of the saints? Or do you not know that the saints will judge the world? And if the world is to be judged by you, are you incompetent to try trivial cases? Do you not know that we are to judge angels? How much more, then, matters pertaining to this life! So if you have such cases, why do you lay them before those who have no standing in the

---

duce the Nephilim. Some have suggested that this is why Paul told women to cover their heads, as opposed to being called to proper behaviour due to an awareness of the holy angels. In the light of other texts noted about awareness of the holy angels being required, this reading is unlikely.

church? I say this to your shame. Can it be that there is no one
among you wise enough to settle a dispute between the brothers?
(1 Cor 6:1–5)

Here angels are put forward in the midst of an argument, and as
a wake-up call to the Corinthians. The Corinthians lacked wisdom,
judgement, and clarity of vision, blindly taking their fellow believers
to court, being unloving to them, and a bad witness to those around.
Angels live the perfect godly life, this we have seen. How on earth will
you then, Corinthian, with your selfish and grasping judgmental attitudes, judge them? How humiliating it would be to stand in court as
the lawyer, and have yourself exposed as a lawbreaker by the one you
are cross-examining! If you are judging the world, that is one thing
since it is fallen and sinful, but judging the holy host of heaven is something else entirely. In Jesus' words, we should learn how to "judge with
right judgement" (John 7:24).

One last aspect to consider is that angels can promote the godly
life to us, by speaking directly into, or stirring, our hearts and souls. We
looked at this earlier, and have returned to it at various points, showing
that just as fallen angels can influence for the negative, holy angels can
also do so for the positive.

REDEMPTION

In this context, redemption does not mean salvation, but a returning
to the journey God has for you, with renewed vigour and vision, after
a traumatic experience of some kind. It does not restore the loss (that
would be healing), but renews the journey on a transformed basis. It
works towards spiritual advancement, and recovering a positive outlook
on life. It also suggests a move from passive into active in our lives.

Obviously, the concept of a journeying guardian angel, who walks
alongside you through life, and so with you as you go into the next stage
of life, can be reassuring, and provide a platform to launch from. You are
not alone! The more detailed issue of guidance will be considered later,
but the angelic companion who guides and advises, who prays for and
with you, and who stands beside you in times of trouble, builds into a
developed idea of redeeming angelic ministry and guardian angels.

Rev 12 also may provide a context. Following the description of
the heavenly battle, and Satan's ejection from heaven, is a well-known

passage in which we read that the saints overcame Satan by *the blood of the Lamb, the word of their testimony, and not loving their lives unto death* (12:11). Alongside the victorious battling of the angels, individuals have their own role and pressures in the journey; angels and men journey and battle together. This recognizes both the battle and the ultimate answer in Christ, but also the reality of the call to perseverance and active journeying in the face of problems.

One can also focus on the assurance of salvation at the end, and that our journey through life, with all its ups and downs, will have a positive outcome. Raising our heads, the renewed vision of paradise and the heavenly life in the society of angels, can be a motivation in the present. It will be worth it in the end, even if in the very moment of "now," we do not see or feel it. We get up, and begin our walk with God again, since the final destination is worth the struggle. These various threads are supremely shown in one single story, Jacob's passage of life to the angelic ladder, and his new journey afterwards.

Jacob's Story

Twins Jacob and Esau had a rocky relationship, it seems, almost from the womb, and throughout their childhoods' their parents each favoured a different one (Gen 25:24–28). During their younger years, Esau recklessly sold Jacob his birthright for some soup, which Jacob gladly let him do (Gen 25:29–34). Jacob then proceeded to ensure that this mistake was not reversed. In Gen 27 we read that Jacob, perhaps on the premise of the birthright he now owned, deceived his father Isaac into giving him his final blessing—a blessing which should have been Esau's. Jacob therefore took Esau's birthright and blessing (27:36), and with no way of redressing this, Esau began to hate Jacob and planned to kill him. With such conflict boiling, Jacob was sent away for his own safety to start a new life elsewhere, and it was while on this journey he had the vision of the angelic ladder (28:10–22).

Jacob reached this place of vision in the midst of much personal turmoil, most of which was self-inflicted. He was at a crossroads in his life. What was he to do next? This vision was crucial to Jacob. It told him he was not alone, that God was with him and would bless him, and that his angels worked on earth. It was also a crucial event because it told Jacob that God's presence and God's angels were not limited to visiting single, specific holy places, but God and his angels could meet him at any location. While later generations would cite this as a holy place, and it became a specific centre of worship, it was also a sign of the on-going and ever-present protection and presence of God, wherever Jacob may go, as later meetings with God and his angels in other places testified to (28:15). God's presence and the Gate of Heaven can be opened anywhere on earth, and also upon anybody! Jacob's response to this was to dedicate his life to God (28:20–22), and to vow to live in a way pleasing to him. He also resolved to look for peace with his family.

However, good intentions are not always fully followed through. Deep changes of heart are sometimes slow to be totally realised, and Jacob's less than godly ways continued. True, God blessed him with children and wealth, and allowed a level of restoration between Jacob and Esau to happen, yet he did not always protect Jacob from the results of his own deviousness. Nevertheless, and very importantly, on two occasions God's undeserved grace was shown to him, and Jacob was spoken to by angels.

The first time was in a dream (31:11). In this dream Jacob was told how he was to counteract Laban's devious tactics, and so Jacob was recompensed for Laban's long standing scheming. This allowed him to leave the area with wealth, able to support himself and his family, and start a new life elsewhere. (God himself had told him, not through an angel, to leave. God can choose the methods he wants, when he wants, as suits him best.)

However, Jacob still had Esau to contend with. Prior to this meeting, angels met him once again (32:1). Quite what was said we are not told, but directly afterwards Jacob has a decisive plan of action which allows him to meet Esau peacefully. Just as angels directed his ways before, they did so again here. The meeting with Esau went well, and from this point Jacob's life changed. He wrestled with God,[25] and was from then on called Israel. Angels remained an on-going sign of God's presence and guidance in his life, and Israel/Jacob recognised this at the end of his life. When he blessed Joseph, he said: "The God before whom my fathers Abraham and Isaac walked, the God who has been my shepherd all my life long to this day, *the angel who has redeemed me from all evil*, bless the boys; and in them let my name be carried on, and the name of my fathers Abraham and Isaac; and let them grow into a multitude in the midst of the earth" (Gen 48:15–16).

25. Gen 32:24–30.

"The angel who has redeemed me from all evil." What an intriguing phrase. What does redeem mean?[26] Is it the redemption given by the one true redeemer, Jesus Christ? Some commentators say that some of the angelic visitations to Jacob were christophanies. For example, after the "man" (called an "angel" in Hos 12:4) wrestled with him, Jacob said he had seen God face to face. Thus the angel who redeems is actually the Redeemer God, Jesus Christ. The Hebrew here has a rich sense: to redeem, to act as kinsman-redeemer, to avenge, to ransom. The primary Scriptures that deal with this principle are Lev 25, Num 35, Deut 19, and Ruth 4. Redemption is simply deliverance from some sort of bondage, a release of someone or something from an alien power that has a claim on it. The biblical idea of redemption also involves the deliverer and what he must do to effect the deliverance. This concept links the two as a close family member who does the delivering. Yes, Jesus is the ultimate kinsman redeemer, yet others can serve as kinsman redeemers on a human level, like Boaz for Ruth, or, as in our story, as an angel for Jacob. But here we see Jacob focus his devotion and thanksgiving to God, who sometimes appeared to him as angel.

This blessing provides a book-end to a section which began with the angelic ladder, where God with his angels met Jacob. It ends with God, and his "theophanic" redeeming angel. In between, God speaks with Jacob directly, meets Jacob as the angel of the Lord, and also guides him by means of his ministering angels. Jacob's words seem to have a double echo, primarily to *the* Angel, but also to God's angels.

Therefore, Jacob's vision of the angelic ladder was pivotal. Here he saw that God, by his angels, reached down to touch lives and change their courses for the better. Jacob experienced this twice, and then at the end of his life restates this truth. God, either by his direct word or intervention, or by his angels, redeems lives in the sense of putting them on the right path—God's path, a path with a divinely chosen and shaped destiny. Jacob had a life-long journey of trouble and problems. However, the turning point was the vision of God's angelic ladder, and from thereon in, despite blips and stumbles (which are the norm of a fallen life), Jacob's life was turned around, redeemed, and the angelic presence at key points in his life drove him onward.

---

26. Redeemed—Heb Gen 48:16, *haggoēl 'oti* (lit, "the one redeeming me"); LXX root: *ruomai* / ῥύομαι.

Angels are given by grace, given by God to people who do not deserve their presence, let alone God's presence! They can be a sign of simple undeserved blessing and favour, for which to be thankful. Angels walk with us through life as sustaining companions and as examples of the holy life. Jacob experienced this first hand, so did Daniel, and later the apostles. Not always in the same way, and not always in the expected way, but they were sustained and protected by angels, and for that they were thankful, as we should also be.

So, sustained on our journey, our next need is to know that we are heading in the right direction. Being sustained only to walk the wrong way, going down dead-end roads, or off the edge of cliffs, is of little use. God knows this, and so uses his angels to keep us on the right path, and it is this issue of guidance that we will now consider.

7

ANGELS AND GUIDING

GUIDING IS THAT VITAL ministry which brings wisdom and enlightenment concerning what one ought to do when faced with a difficult problem of choosing between various courses of thought or action.[1] It is the response to the cry of "*What do I do?*"

The four aspects of guidance are, first *advice-giving* (including words of discipline), which is the true knowledge and insight given by a wise counsellor specifically for a troubled person's situation. The second, "*devil-craft*," is the ability to stand against Satan. This happens through avoiding isolation and can also include exorcism and the removal of demonic oppression. Third is *listening*, to clarify a situation or to allow a troubled person to unburden themselves. Finally there is simple decision making, to encourage and promote wise and helpful decisions and courses of action.[2]

But what does this look like? Guidance, in its simplest forms, is just telling people where to go, or not to go, what to do or not to do. The Israelites following the angel in the pillar of cloud in the desert was an active and positive example of this, and the cherubim blocking entry back into Eden (Gen 3:24), a more passive and negative example. Angels do offer general guidance, but let us look at how they guide more specifically and directly.

ADVICE GIVING

Giving advice and relaying information is the most obvious and well known of all angelic ministries. For example, both Mary and Joseph were met by, and guided by angels on more than one occasion, as were

1. Clebsch and Jaekle, *Pastoral*, 49–50.
2. Ibid., 54.

Elizabeth, Zachariah, and the shepherds.[3] These angels manifested themselves in bodily forms, in dreams, and through audible voices. But there
are plenty of other biblical examples beyond these well known ones.

True advice-giving will involve words of discipline and teaching,
including instruction against what the person may naturally want to do.
When an angel met Hagar, she was asked what her problem was, and
then told to return to her mistress, to live humbly under her roof. (Gen
16:9). Similarly, Abraham was told to not sacrifice Isaac by the word of
an angel. However, one of the best examples of discipline is Balaam's
meeting with an angel:

> Then the LORD opened the eyes of Balaam, and he saw the angel
> of the LORD standing in the way, with his drawn sword in his
> hand. And he bowed down and fell on his face. And the angel of
> the LORD said to him, "Why have you struck your donkey these
> three times? Behold, I have come out to oppose you because your
> way is perverse before me. The donkey saw me and turned aside
> before me these three times. If she had not turned aside from me,
> surely just now I would have killed you and let her live." Then
> Balaam said to the angel of the LORD," I have sinned, for I did not
> know that you stood in the road against me. Now therefore, if it
> is evil in your sight, I will turn back." And the angel of the LORD
> said to Balaam, "Go with the men, but speak only the word that
> I tell you." So Balaam went on with the princes of Balak. (Num
> 22:31–35)

Initially, Balaam was blind to what was going on, but when his eyes
were opened and he saw the angel, his entire demeanour changed. The
angel disciplined him about beating his donkey, declaring Balaam's actions perverse. Angels are sent to discipline and stop people doing wrong
things. The angel then commended the donkey for doing what Balaam
could not do—having the spiritual awareness to know God was moving
in the place!—and by the actions of the donkey Balaam's life was saved.
If the donkey had not done what it did, the ultimate act of discipline
was going to happen—Balaam was to be killed. Now we see the vital
postscript to this meeting.

Balaam's reaction to the discipline of the angel was recognition of
wrong, confession and repentance, and then a willingness to put it right
and obey the words of the angel. Balaam then became open to the voice

---

3. E.g., Matt 1:20ff.; 2:13ff.; Luke 1:11ff., 26ff.; 2:8ff.

of God and the Spirit of God (Num 24:2). He met with God (Num 23:4, 16), and he spoke his words as directed (Num 23:5, 16). Balaam's series of oracles were bravely and clearly said, provoking the anger of Balak (Num 24:10), yet he could do no other. The meeting with the angel had re-orientated Balaam's view of the world and God, and changed his life—for example, he did not resort to sorcery as at other times (Num 24:1). The meeting and correction from the angel, led Balaam into a relationship with God and for him to be used by God.

A similar story is found in Judges, where an angel went from Gilgal to Bochim. After recounting the blessing of God in the exodus, and exposing the false worship and idolatry of the people, the angel says: "'So now I say, I will not drive them out before you, but they shall become thorns in your sides, and their gods shall be a snare to you.' As soon as the angel of the LORD spoke these words to all the people of Israel, the people lifted up their voices and wept. And they called the name of that place Bochim. And they sacrificed there to the LORD" (Judg 2:3–5). Truth was stated, followed by words of discipline and correction, which led to repentance, and sacrifice to God. God used his angel as a disciplinary spur to the people to change their behaviour and return to him.

Advice giving is also the true knowledge and insight given by a wise counsellor specifically for a troubled person's situation. Take, for example, Daniel's meetings with Gabriel. Daniel was given an uncomfortable vision of two angels talking together, and at the end one speaks with Daniel (Dan 8:1–14). Daniel did not understand the vision, but Gabriel was assigned to explain it (Dan 8:16). It is worth noting that at the end of the explanation, Daniel, while more enlightened, is still deeply troubled (Dan 8:27)—receiving advice does not always mean instant peace of mind or heart, but may give one something further to wrestle with.

This pattern is echoed in Dan 9 where Daniel, in sackcloth and ashes, was pleading and fasting (v. 3), clearly troubled by the situation God's people were in. During his prayer, Gabriel came to him. In this instance, God sent his angel with an immediacy which must have comforted Daniel incredibly. We then read: "[Gabriel] made me understand, speaking with me and saying, 'O Daniel, I have now come out to give you insight and understanding. At the beginning of your pleas for mercy a word went out, and I have come to tell it to you, for you are greatly loved. Therefore consider the word and understand the vision'" (Dan 9:22–23).

This short passage speaks of so much more than simple revelation, but also of God and his ministry to his people, by his angels. Gabriel was sent with haste when Daniel began to pray, to give insight, understanding and to affirm to Daniel that he is greatly loved by God. Great affirmation though was not enough, and Gabriel still instructs Daniel to consider the word and understand the vision. This is the truth and compassion of God, affirmed by his angel, to his beloved.

Finally, advice-giving also seeks to bring the person into a situation which will be conducive to their welfare. The clearest example of this is evangelism, since a relationship with Christ is always the best start point for anybody. The result of entering his church and body is wider and greater access to the wisdom of God through other Christians. It also begins to shape one's life into positive directions—a more subtle and implicit form of guidance, but guidance to be sure. The case of Balaam shows how angels are a part of directing people to God, however the easiest way of demonstrating the angelic role in evangelism is to look at the presentation we see in Acts. Of the seven angelic appearances, all either implicitly or explicitly, promoted the gospel of Jesus Christ. This is, again, a good example of how singular angelic acts have numerous further effects. There is an interesting mirror image of the commission from Christ in Acts 1 to the disciples, where the angels are acting in line with what Christ said: "You will be my witnesses in Jerusalem, and in all Judea and Samaria, and to the ends of the earth" (Acts 1:8).

The gospel would cross all religious, cultural and geographical boundaries. So, how did the angels help this process?

1. In Acts 1:10–11 the two angels (figures in white) effectively tell the men, "Don't just stand there, get on with what Jesus instructed you to do!" The disciples' calling was not to stare at the sky, but to wait for the Spirit to come, and so to be clothed with power from on high.

2. An angel freed the apostles from jail and then told them to go back to the temple to preach Life, to preach Jesus; but who was this to? They were to go to the temple, so the call was to go to Jews—local and otherwise—in Jerusalem (Acts 5:19–21).

3. An angel guided Andrew to the Ethiopian, so he could tell him of Christ (Acts 8:26–40). Andrew found the Ethiopian on the road going out of Jerusalem, heading south to Gaza. Not only

was this probably broadening the preaching of the gospel to the Jewish Diaspora (or maybe Gentile God-fearers), more significantly it was direction to preach to, and baptise, a eunuch. Eunuchs were excluded from the temple and the Mosaic Law (Lev 22:24; Deut 23:1), and for the angel to direct Andrew to this eunuch broadened even further the tent of the gospel.

4.   An angel met Cornelius, and told him to speak to Peter, who would then tell him the gospel (Acts 10:1–6). Besides the fact that the angel, on behalf of God, affirmed the God-fearing life of love, prayer, and charity shown by Cornelius, the angel also directed Cornelius to where his God-fearing faith could be made complete. Peter had to battle to not only accept that a Gentile could become a full member of the people of God, without being a Jewish convert, but also one has to note that Cornelius was one of the army of the hated occupiers. I would suspect that Peter had to wrestle long and hard with the idea that an angel of God came to a military Gentile and affirmed him instead of judging him! One also suspects that if the angel had not directed Cornelius to Peter, then Peter may well not have fully understood the vision he got, nor its application nor purpose. The angel's presence was not only a testimony that God approved of Cornelius, but was the catalyst to move the gospel further beyond the boundaries of Israel.

5.   In the light of James' death at Herod's hand (Acts 12:1–2), Peter's release from jail by an angel also saved him from death (Acts 12:3–11). The true importance of this would only later be seen: for example, Peter's subsequent role in the Jerusalem Council (allowing the widening of the mission to Gentiles (Acts 15)), indicates how significant this release was in the furthering the gospel, especially for Paul and Barnabas, but also for Peter himself. Freeing Peter allowed the continuation of the spreading of the gospel to the Gentiles all over the known world.

6.   An angel assured Paul that he would stand before Nero (Acts 27:23–25), and in the light of his other speeches throughout Acts, it is unlikely that Paul would not have given Nero a clear gospel presentation. Here we see an angel, not only reaffirming to Paul the promise of God that the gospel would get to Rome,

but also encouraging him in the midst of a terrible situation where he may have thought he would die. No, the angel says, you will not die! Be of good heart and trust God. The gospel would now go to Rome, the hub from which the ends of the known earth could be reached.

The one exception to this pattern of explicit promotion of the gospel was when an angel killed Herod for his pride and arrogance (Acts 12:20–23). Yet even here when one considers that Herod had started to kill the apostles (James), removing him from power was allowed the apostles to live and work without threat, to spread the gospel far and wide.

Therefore, in contrast to more New Age or Spiritualist understandings of angels, the biblical presentation of post-Pentecost angelic ministry will always, either directly or indirectly, lead to the promotion and advancement of the gospel. The idea of angels simply appearing for the benefit or whim of an individual to answer questions about one's business concerns, the origins of dolphins, or to show you who your next lover might be, is not the reason for their ministry. Angelic ministry will always promote a positive spiritual reaction within, and if the post-Pentecost pattern is consistent, this will always point in the direction of Christ.

People often fear angelic guidance, and worry that if they have a meeting with, or message from, an angel, they may be misled by Satan, an angel of light (2 Cor 11:14). How can we know that an angel is giving good guidance? How do we know that it is not a demon wanting to mislead? How can one have the wisdom to discern this? Often, through the centuries, people have panicked over this question and ultimately refused to take seriously any angelic message. Yet, with what you have just read the discernment process is actually very simple. Post-Pentecost all angelic ministry is directed toward Christ, to his glory, and conversions into his kingdom and Life. So simply ask, is the angelic message glorifying Christ and advancing his kingdom in people's lives? A demon would direct you anywhere except towards Christ. An angel of God would never direct you anywhere but toward Christ. Discernment is simple, so do not fear angelic guidance. Christ is the plumb-line.

DEVIL CRAFT

Devil-craft is the ability to stand against Satan, either by rejecting Satan's temptation or driving out demonic influence from one's life. We have already considered angels and demonic oppression in chapter 5 on healing, but richer detail will be given here as to their wider role in this context.

The classic example which Christians have used throughout history to illustrate devil craft is described in Tobit, where the Archangel Raphael heals illnesses and binds demons, which then draws forth praise and a commitment to a righteous life. However, unlike this story from the Apocrypha which is neatly packaged into one concise unit, the biblical evidence spreads out over the pages of the Two Testaments.

Broadly, the idea of angels strengthening people against temptation links to the idea of positive angelic influence upon the heart, either by stirring, guidance, or actual direct instruction. One might reflect therefore on the angelic ministry to Christ himself when in Gethsemane, where in his distress, an angel came to *strengthen* him (Luke 22:43), as well as the ministry given after Satan's temptations in the wilderness. (Matt 4:11). However, Clebsch and Jaekle's definition says that it also happens through avoiding isolation and ensuring that one is with other believers, in the church and under the word. How do angels stop people being isolated and lonely? There are a number of stories which show this.

Looking at the life of Hagar, in which she had many issues and hurdles to contend with, we see a tendency in her to isolate herself and run away from problems. However, as Gen 16 says, God had a plan for her, her child, and all her subsequent descendents—to make them into a great nation. It was not God's plan for her or her child to die. So we see the angel telling Hagar to return to Abraham and Sarah (Gen 16:7–9). This would not have been an easy option, and the later re-emerging battle within the family group testifies to that, but at least, within that group, Hagar would be safe. The angel appeared, letting Hagar know she was not alone, and then guided her back to the safety of Abraham's household.

After Hagar returned, she had Ishmael, but conflict reared its ugly head again after Sarah had Isaac. Hagar and Ishmael were driven away (Gen 21:9–21), and once more the angel found them. However, this time, the angel did not tell them to return, but his presence nonetheless meant that they were not alone. Instead the angel provided what they needed (water), and subsequently God allowed them to build a new life elsewhere (Gen 21:20–21). This second event again showed Hagar that she was not alone and unheard, and God's angel would come to her in her distress. In both instances, isolation was challenged and reversed, bring Hagar and Ishmael into a community. This role of building relationships and stopping isolation is reaffirmed a couple of chapters later, when an angel reappears. God tells Abraham he will send his angel on a journey before his servant to pave his way, and find a wife for his son. Angels are sent before one on a journey to prepare the way, to smooth the way of success, even to help people find soul mates (Gen 24:7, 40).

A different example is Elijah in 1 Kgs 19:1–8. He was weak and panicked, and in this state he ran into the wilderness alone. He had just defeated the prophets of Baal and seen God's incredible power, yet when faced with Jezebel's threats his strength ebbs and fades. Satan would have seen what God could do through Elijah, and he knew he had to stop him. Jezebel's words would have achieved that very nicely. By sowing seeds of doubt and fear, and driving Elijah into isolation in the desert, he then became impotent and useless. This was not Elijah's role or destiny. He was on the wrong path. In the midst of his depression and wanting to end his life, an angel came, touched him, and woke him (vs. 5, 7). And the angel did this twice. Elijah was provided with food and water for a journey to the Mount of God by the angel, but the angel also *touched* him. (Heb: *naga*: LXX root: *apto* / απτω).

This word for touched has a broad meaning, and can either mean a soft or a hard touch, gentle or not. However, when it is applied to angels or angelic figures the word never has the harsher sense. Its only other occurrences in 1 and 2 Kings speak of the cherubim's wing touching the temple, and when the dead man touched the bones of Elijah he came alive again—a touch which heals (1 Kgs 6:27; 2 Kgs 13:21)! This life-giving touch is also shown by its use in Daniel, when the angels or fiery figure gently raises and encourages Daniel from the floor after he has collapsed (Dan 8:18; 10:10; 10:16, 18). It is also the word used to describe when God touches people to give them gifts, strength or comfort, the most striking occasions being when God touched Jeremiah's mouth to allow him to preach, and when the angel touched Isaiah's lips with the coal to cleanse him (Jer 1:9; Isa 6:7). More poignantly, it is the touch that Jesus gave the leper to heal him in Matt 8:3.

The touch here is one of comfort and strengthening. Many people in the midst of loneliness and despair value the loving touch from somebody who cares for them. A comforting hug, a shoulder to cry upon, or simply one hand holding another. All these forms of touch provide a comfort and reassurance in desperate times, and can communicate even more powerfully than words ever could in that moment. The angel could have called to wake Elijah up or shaken him, but instead it was a touch. This is not the word for touch (strike) that Peter got in Acts 12:7. This is gentler. Touch is a real physical tangible statement that you are not alone. The angel provided for Elijah in his isolation, not only physically but also emotionally, so he could journey for forty days and meet with God who would renew his faith and spirit and set him once again on the right path. Angels will sustain us on many levels as we journey to God, and ensure we are not alone and isolated, a sitting duck for Satan's attack.

For a New Testament example, one can again consider in Acts 12 the angel that released Peter from jail. The angel took him to the praying disciples, away from the threat of Herod. The angel both protected Peter from Herod's murderous ways, and also returned him to the fold of believers. He was now both physically and spiritually in a safe place.

Finally, exorcism and removal of demonic oppression is also a key part of *devil-craft*. This was described in detail in the chapter on healing, but it is worth recapping some of that material here. We know of the great act of exorcism by Michael and his angels in Rev 12, that Michael's work was done in the name of the Lord and not in his own name or strength, and that sometimes, as in Dan 10, battles with demons mean a time delay between heaven hearing and responding to prayer and us seeing the outworking on earth.

All these stand as truths that angels fight for us, protect us, and remove demonic oppression from our lives. Yet there is one other example of this which slightly reverses the action, but retains the same basic result. Until now we have seen angels remove the demonic from people. In this last case, we see an angel removing people from the demonic, the good from the evil, to allow the good to go free and the evil to be destroyed. Angels removing people from the oppression of evil and the demonic is just as liberating as the action moving the other way, and this is shown in Gen 19:1–22. The story of Lot and the destruction of Sodom is well known, but to pause and look at exactly what the angels did, sheds new light on the story. The moral state of the city is clear from the story, as is the will of the inhabitants to corrupt others when they had the chance. The mission of the angels was to ensure that Lot and his family left the city before it was destroyed. The angels protected Lot by not only striking the people blind, but also by dragging Lot back into the house, and closing the door to escape the men (19:10–11). Further, in getting Lot and his family away from Sodom, it was an act of removing them from demonic oppression, an evil culture, and the coming judgment.

Angels will come and protect those God promises protection to, even if the people are not particularly honorable or decent. Even a cursory glance at Lot's behaviour shows he too had been deeply corrupted by the city he was living in. Nevertheless, the angels, in obedience to God's mercy, protected and rescued this family of dubious moral character. Angels are not proud, but they are obedient. They stand solely by the grace of God, not of their own strength, and they know this from first-hand experience. 2 Pet 2:4 speaks of angels who had sinned and fallen, possibly alluding to Gen 6 and the Nephilim. The damnation of this section of the angelic society is known and certain, yet seven verses later we then read:

> Angels, though greater in might and power [than arrogant humans], do not pronounce a blasphemous judgment against them before the Lord. (2 Pet 2:11)

This comment is made in the light of the previous verse where arrogant men are said to have rejected the godly authority placed over them, which implicitly includes angels—since those who *despise authority* are those who *slander celestial beings*. In contrast, angels know their places, and do not denounce the wicked out of hand. Not only is this the role of God, but perhaps they also know all too well the grace they have received, and which other angels have not due to their choices and conduct. They have seen the consequences of the grace-less, God-rejecting life of the fallen angels. They have seen their community forever and permanently ripped apart by sin. And so they work with the painful first-hand knowledge of the destruction that rebellion against God brings, for the restoration and protection of our lives and communities, wanting to serve God as best they can, to resist the assault of evil that wants to pound God's people and his world. This is also why angels rejoice when a sinner repents, since they see what the future holds for those who do not. Their angelic brethren—fallen and eternally separated from God—

are before their eyes. Their personal experience of a torn society drives them not to want us humans to experience it too. Yet again, angels seem not so far from us. We can learn from, and emulate this service of these heavenly beings, who like us were reconciled to the Father by the blood of Christ's cross (Col 1:16–20, esp. 20),[4] ceaselessly serving their Creator, for the benefit of his creation, out of a knowledge of his undeserved love and grace, and the blessed future he offers. This is no mission done by impassive, inscrutable beings unemotionally led by the Spirit, but one of godly, obedient beings driven by a living, personal awareness of what a life without Christ will ultimately mean for us.

LISTENING

Listening is important for many reasons. For example, you cannot not guide properly unless you know what the problem is. Alternatively, allowing a troubled person to unburden themselves in a safe context can be very helpful. Listening can also allow someone to open their heart, without fear, and create an atmosphere where sharing is possible. Listening is a necessary skill in pastoral care.

Demonstrating the listening skills of angels from Scripture is not straightforward (though the same can be said of the listening skills of humans). It is very difficult to pin down evidence for it. However, what I think that we can show from the Bible is that angels, generally, have good pastoral communication skills, of which listening is one. And because angels have these skills, we can be assured that angels will not go off half-cocked, or only get part of the story, or misread situations and so then provide bad advice and guidance.

Angels listen to God. Not only that, they seem to be in a council of sorts which surrounds God. There is an angelic heavenly council that God speaks with, but it is clearly God who rules and runs this council. There is no sense of democracy under the Lord Almighty: "Let the heavens praise your wonders, O LORD, your faithfulness in the assembly of the holy ones! For who in the skies can be compared to the LORD? Who among the heavenly beings is like the LORD, a God greatly to be feared in the council of the holy ones, and awesome above all who are around him? O LORD God of hosts, who is mighty as you are, O LORD, with your faithfulness all around you?" (Ps 89:5–8).

---

4. More detail about this is given in ch. 8—Angels and Reconciliation.

And since there is no democracy, there is no chance that a wrong decision will ever result from the discussions on this council. Despite this, we see in Job 1 that some on the council are less than enamored with what God is doing, and use the council meetings as an opportunity to denounce God's work and faithful people. There are discussions, and it also seems that there is some scope for those on the council or in the chamber to come up with ideas, which God then agrees to, or not, and, if he agrees, ensures will work:

> And Micaiah said, "Therefore hear the word of the LORD: I saw the LORD sitting on his throne, and all the host of heaven standing beside him on his right hand and on his left; and the LORD said, 'Who will entice Ahab, that he may go up and fall at Ramoth-gilead?' And one said one thing, and another said another. Then a spirit came forward and stood before the LORD, saying, 'I will entice him.' And the LORD said to him, 'By what means?' And he said, 'I will go out, and will be a lying spirit in the mouth of all his prophets.' And he said, 'You are to entice him, and you shall succeed; go out and do so.'" (1 Kgs 22:19–22)

The spirit suggested the idea, and God agreed to it, saying that the plan would work. Now, if God allows ideas from a spirits (or even from Satan, cf. Job 1), how much more would he allow ideas from his holy angels? God will not be deflected by bad counsel, but graciously allows angels to come up with ideas—ideas which God would have already had. Like prayer, God knows what we need before we pray, but nonetheless he wants us to pray and be involved with him and his Life. And when we also reflect upon the other passages like Matt 18:10, where angels stand before God on our behalf, we build up a powerful picture of a council, wonderfully led by God, full of wise and obedient angels, who, after discussing and offering opinions, then do his will perfectly. My point is that angels are not automatons. They know what they are doing when they are sent out by God, and why. Because they know that God sanctions the action, it is therefore right and trustworthy, and to be pursued until completed.

Angels also listen to and converse with people—they do not simply download information at them. However, when people meet an angel, if it is recognised as an angel, they are rarely in a place to be open and objective, or communicate well. Zechariah was startled and gripped with fear (Luke 1:12), Mary was troubled, not by the appearance but the angel's words (Luke 1:29), and Daniel was literally knocked off his feet when he met Gabriel (Dan 8:17–18). In these instances angels must have been aware of how the person was feeling at that moment and communicated appropriately. Angels must have the communication skills to overcome the fear, panic, and confusion their presence evokes. It is comforting, therefore, to know that it is usual for the first words of an angel to be, "Do not fear!"[5] To Mary, Gabriel said: "Greetings, O favoured one, the Lord is with you!"

As noted previously, this simple sentence is packed with subtleties. We see a warm welcome (Greetings!); we see a statement of who Mary is to reassure her that is not a negative visit of judgment (O favoured one), and an assurance of God's presence not only in the angel, but with Mary herself (the Lord is with you). It is a well crafted and well pitched opening statement that, along with Gabriel's use of Mary's name to create a personal connection and relationship, is designed to reduce her anxiety and fear, and allow her to hear what he was going to say.

It is also important that both Zachariah and Mary replied to, and questioned, the angel. There is no sense that the angel had just come to deliver a monologue and leave. The angel listened to the words, understanding their meaning and nuance. Just look at how differently Gabriel reacted to the questions by Zechariah and Mary. Again, when looking at Matt 28:4–7 when Mary Magdalene and the women met the angel at the tomb, one sees how the angel put them at ease to receive the information. The guards had fear, and I assume the women too, but it was to the women the angel turned, knowing why they were there, and knowing what to tell them, while being fully aware of the fear induced by his presence. While not technically an act of listening, it is very much an act of pastoral awareness which allowed appropriate guidance to be given. Eighty percent of communication is non-verbal, and so listening includes observing a situation and body language as much as it does hearing words. And on this last point, it is important to note that the angel was *sitting* on the rock. He was not standing tall, at his full height with all the presence and awe that would create. Angels are aware of both their presence and body language.

Similarly, Gen 21 echoes this, where Hagar, lost, troubled, and wandering in the desert, is heard by the angel of God: "The angel of God called to Hagar from heaven and said to her, 'What troubles you, Hagar?

---

5. E.g., Luke 1:13, 30; 2:10; 28:5; Acts 27:23–24.

Fear not, for God has heard the voice of the boy where he is. Up! Lift up the boy, and hold him fast with your hand, for I will make him into a great nation'" (Gen 21:17–18).

The angel asks what troubles her. But surely he knew anyway. Nevertheless, he invites communication and offers consolation. Angels invite communication and conversation. Yet, I hear you cry, all of these examples focus mainly on good communication skills, not necessarily listening as such. This is true, but good communication skills require good listening skills, and it is in Judges where we see a great angelic example of this:

> Now the angel of the LORD came and sat under the terebinth at Ophrah, which belonged to Joash the Abiezrite, while his son Gideon was beating out wheat in the winepress to hide it from the Midianites. And the angel of the LORD appeared to him and said to him, "The LORD is with you, O mighty man of valour." And Gideon said to him, "Please, sir if the LORD is with us, why then has all this happened to us? And where are all his wonderful deeds that our fathers recounted to us, saying, 'Did not the LORD bring us up from Egypt?' But now the LORD has forsaken us and given us into the hand of Midian." (Judg 6:11–13)

Once again notice the sitting posture of the angel, which allowed Gideon to approach without fear. Gideon unloaded a lot of criticism and doubt upon the angel. Where is God in this? What is God doing? This makes no sense! Unlike the doubt of Zechariah which elicited judgment, in this instance the angel of the Lord listened and responded with the words of God saying: "Go in this might of yours and save Israel from the hand of Midian; do not I send you?" (Judg 6:14). Gideon then responded with further weak doubts: "Please, Lord, how can I save Israel? Behold, my clan is the weakest in Manasseh, and I am the least in my father's house" (Judg 6:15). The angel of the LORD replied and said: "But I will be with you, and you shall strike the Midianites as one man" (Judg 6:16).

Here is a conversation where the angel listened to and bore with Gideon's doubt and questions. The angel knew the concerns and problems going on in Gideon's heart (latterly worries about meeting God's angel, but initially his wider situation) and reassured him at each stage— God would go with him. Similar conversations were had by Daniel, and the same pattern emerges. Daniel, struck dumb and shocked by the encounters, is gently supported and helped to understand the vision or message brought by the angels.

DECISION-MAKING

As with many of these categories, boundaries blur, so much of this is covered elsewhere. Nevertheless, more can be said. *Decision-making* is the simple ministry of giving wisdom and sound advice to help someone make the right choice. But to take advice, you must trust the one giving advice. We know angels are wise and we can trust their words, but can they convey that trustworthiness to us so we will do as they say, even when our instincts would say otherwise? How reliable are angels, since God can charge them with folly (Job 4:18)? This is good question to ask before embarking on this section. One could begin by looking at Gal 1:8, where Paul says that even if an angel of God gives you a different gospel, don't obey it. Could an angel proclaim a false gospel? No. This is simply hyperbole to make a point. Paul cites an example of a messenger who doesn't get it wrong, who doesn't twist things, who is holy and honest, and then says that *even if* such a trustworthy messenger promotes a different gospel (which they wouldn't, anyway), ignore it. Paul's rhetoric works here precisely because angels are wise, reliable, and unfailing in their service of God.

But to look further, angels, despite their enormous knowledge, desire to know more of the things of God. They yearn to look further into the glories of the gospel and the work of God in Christ on earth with humanity (1 Pet 1:12). Therefore they are not resting on their laurels, but constantly seeking more of God to learn more of his will and ways. And this can but only help them in their service of humankind.

We have also seen that angels are holy and converse with God, and then accurately give that message to the person it is intended for, in a way that ensures understanding and comprehension. This foundation (which should be sufficient in itself for us to be assured!), is concretely shown in various ways. But can an angel bringing a message instil confidence in the hearer in order to act on what they are told? We have already seen how in Luke 2 the words of the angel were identified as the words of God, and how the Angel of the LORD can also speak God's words and on his behalf. There is also Jer 23, which, in the context of prophets not speaking God's words to his people, we read of his heavenly council: "For who among them has stood in the council of the LORD to see and to hear his word, or who has paid attention to his word and listened? But if they had stood in my council, then they would have proclaimed my words to my people, and they would have turned them from their evil way, and from the evil of their deeds" (Jer 23:18, 22).

Those in his council proclaim his words to his people in a way that human prophets, sadly, do not, and these words bring changes in how people live and act. Going further we read in 2 Kgs 1 a story of Elijah: The king wished to enquire about his health from Baal-zebub, but an angel came to Elijah: "The angel of the LORD said to Elijah the Tishbite, 'Arise, go up to meet the messengers of the king of Samaria, and say to them, "Is it because there is no God in Israel that you are going to inquire of Baal-zebub, the god of Ekron?" Now therefore, thus says the LORD, "You shall not come down from the bed to which you have gone up, but you shall surely die."' So Elijah went" (2 Kgs 1:3–4).

The angel from God speaks to challenge the king's action, exposing the king's rejection of God in plain terms, and gives words of judgment for Elijah to pronounce. One must trust in the words of an angel to oppose a king in such a way. Elijah trusted the advice and direction given, and went. The king, angry, twice sent soldiers to capture Elijah, and fire consumed both groups. A third group, learning the lesson, spoke with Elijah asking for mercy—but was this a trap, just to lure Elijah out from his safe place? The angel then spoke to Elijah again: "The angel of the LORD said to Elijah, 'Go down with him; do not be afraid of him.' So he arose and went down with him to the king and said to him, 'Thus says the LORD, "Because you have sent messengers to inquire of Baal-zebub, the god of Ekron—is it because there is no God in Israel to inquire of his word?—therefore you shall not come down from the bed to which you have gone up, but you shall surely die"'" (2 Kgs 1:15–16).

The trust in the word of the angel is heightened here. Elijah was to go down to the soldiers and then go with them to the king—into the lion's den! Not only that, once in the middle of this hostile territory, he was to repeat exactly what he had first said, and which had got him into so much trouble. I cannot think that Elijah would choose this course of action, unless he totally trusted the direction given by God's angel. The angel told Elijah what to do, what decision to make, and which course of action to take.

Knowing more of God leads to a godlier life and as angels yearn to know more of God, so should we. We, like them, should hunger so we can love him more, and prepare ourselves for serving his church, and ultimately meeting Christ: "Even angels long to look into these things [i.e., the wonders of the gospel and how God has worked in the world]. So prepare your minds for action. Control yourselves. Put your hope completely in the grace that will be given to you when Jesus Christ returns" (1 Pet 1:12–13). If angels long for more of God, says Peter, so should we, and as a result amend our lifestyles.

Angels give trustworthy guidance, but we should be aware that angelic guidance may not come through startling visions, dreams, and manifestations, but perhaps through less dramatic means. It can be the stranger with the insightful word, the loving member of your church, prompted within by angel to offer words of perceptive discernment, the stirring in your heart toward a course of action, or the inspiration to tell somebody of Christ. Angels can guide wisely, and we should be alive to how God wants to communicate with us through them.

However, we are also called by God to grow in our faith, to mature and learn how to discern for ourselves. God wants us to be wise. We should not therefore expect angels always to provide that wisdom, nor think that we do not have to develop our own relationship with God. As with prayer, God may wish to supplement our wisdom with angelic guidance, or provide special revelation through an angel which is beyond our natural capacities, but he will never wish to replace a relationship with him with angelic guidance. Christ came to reconcile us to the Father, not for us to rely on angels, and it is to reconciliation we now turn for the final part of the jigsaw.

8

ANGELS AND RECONCILIATION

W E HAVE SEEN HOW pastoral care mirrors a journey of the soul. It starts with healing, moves through sustaining and guidance, and now ends with reconciliation. The first three aspects of pastoral care place us on the right path and heading in the right direction. Yet one never wants to journey alone, or go through life with people that one is in conflict with. We all want our passage in life to be as peaceful as possible, and so it is logical that the last part of the jigsaw is the ministry of reconciliation. Not to be confused with the ultimate act of reconciliation through God in Christ, this ministry aims to bring people into a position to be reconciled to both God, and others around them. It is the healing of broken relationships. This can take two basic forms. First is forgiveness, which both restores and heals. Second is discipline to guide, protect, or restrain. So how do angels assist us with reconciliation, forgiveness, and discipline? We have already seen much of the aspect of discipline, and so I will focus on the other two here. To begin with, they help us to worship.

WORSHIP AS RECONCILIATION

As with prayer, the area of worship could sit in any of the chapters, but I choose to place it here. Worship is not singing songs in church, and it is not grovelling to an all-powerful "other." Worship is the place where people turn their eyes away from themselves and their lives, and become orientated to God. God becomes our focus—not ourselves, nor other people, nor the world. In the act of worship one takes the first steps in meeting with God and his reconciling act in Christ. Worship, like prayer, is where we meet with God, and when we meet God we are changed.

God calls us to be changed into his image and likeness. The Westminster Confession says that the chief end of man is to glorify and enjoy God, of which worship is a central aspect. One can hardly say this is wrong. However, what is worship? In many churches today it seems to be limited to singing songs (with varying levels of enthusiasm and abandonment indicating its depth), some prayers, and taking Communion. But worship is far more than this. It is the surrender of the creature to the Creator in all areas of life. William Temple's definition of worship is a reality check, and shows us how soul-deep worship is: "Worship is the submission of all our nature to God. It is the quickening of our conscience by His holiness; the nourishment of our mind with His truth; the purifying of the imagination by His beauty; the opening of the heart to His love; the surrender of the will to His purpose, and all this gathered up in adoration, the most selfless emotion of which our nature is capable."[1]

As we mentioned in chapter 5, worship is the principal act by which we are changed ever more into his image—*as we worship we are changed.*[2] This change is always for the positive, always toward wholeness, and always a process of healing. Worship is important, pastorally, to orientate individual lives to Life: "Worship is central to life, illuminating it from within and bringing awareness of [life's] true character and purpose with which pastoral care is equally concerned."[3]

Therefore by saying that angels assist us, inspire us, and stand by us in worship is saying something far deeper than that we simply sing songs together. By worshipping together, angels help lead us into that transforming relationship with God by which we are profoundly changed. Change begins with reconciliation, first with God then with neighbor (neighbor in the fullest and richest sense of the word). And reconciliation begins with forgiveness. Worship brings into focus an incredible part of pastoral care. So, how do angels help us worship?

We have already seen how angels come to church with us (1 Cor 11:10), but to truly realise that they stand with us every Sunday morning should warn us that worship (and church as a whole) is not a clock-watching exercise. The knowledge of their presence should stir us to take seriously what we do.

---

1. Quoted in: Christou, *Informed Worship,* 14 (Original comment made during a radio programme in 1944).

2. *New Patterns for Worship,* 26ff; cf. Bradshaw, ed., *Companion to Common Worship 2,* 108–20.

3. Campbell, *Dictionary of Pastoral Care,* 299.

But going deeper, God himself associates angels with worship by putting their images into the very design of the tabernacle (Exod 26:1, 31) and upon the Ark of the Covenant (e.g., Exod 25:18–20, 22; 37:7–9); and it is from between the carvings of angels on the lid of the Ark, where God said he would speak to Moses (Exod 25:22; Num 7:89). Cherubim also adorn the temple, and so we see that angels are placed by God at the heart of the place that people were to worship in (1 Kgs 6:23–35). When you came to worship you were confronted with images of angels. We are to recognise they are there, but why? What purpose does it serve to have their images upon the things of God? We are not told explicitly, but there are some indicators.

We are told throughout the Psalms that angels praise God. For example, Pss 29:1; 89:5–8; and Job 38:7 all testify to this. Pss 103 and 148 include their praise in amongst the whole of creation praising God, and it is here we may find the beginning of an answer to the question. There is a regular distinction between different aspects of creation worshipping God. Ps 148 shows this most straightforwardly, being a list of who and what worships. The list begins at the top (the heavens, then angels, then the sun and moon) and works downward, eventually calling all creation to worship God. Now clearly there is a difference between how the rain, the seas, and the cows all worship, and also how humans worship. The logic suggests there would also be a difference between angels and humans.

Ps 103 echoes this flow of thought, but shows us the great distinction. In Ps 103:1–19 we see the frailty and sinfulness of humans exposed, so while it begins in verses 1–2 with the classic cry of *Praise the Lord, O my soul*, it then moves into the problems that life brings us. Humans, as broken beings, trip up, sin, wander off course, and end up as transient as dust and flowers in a storm. God, compassionate, faithful and loving, corrects human errors and lifts us up, but the fact that humanity needs lifting up in the first place is significant. The Psalm ends, however, with a short and simple statement, that contrasts the previous 18 verses: "The LORD has established his throne in the heavens, and his kingdom rules over all. Praise the LORD, you his angels, you mighty ones who do his bidding, who obey his word. Praise the LORD, all his heavenly hosts, you his servants who do his will" (Ps 103:19–21).

There is no sense of vacillation with angels, and no need for eighteen verses of definition and defence of human worship and the human condition. Angels do his bidding and obey his word. Solid in what they do, they are unshakable in their work for him, and praise of him.

Nothing more is said to add to this until we reach the last book of the New Testament and the amazing vision of heaven and history in Revelation. Revelation gives us many examples of hymns of praise and worship, and it shows us what heavenly worship is like, in contrast to the Psalms which show us what human worship looks like.

In Revelation there are eight occasions of praise to God and/or the Lamb. The first is on the earth (1:4–6), from the pen of John by way of introduction to the book. The other seven are in heaven, and are engaged in by various groups, and this heavenly worship is contrasted with the idolatry of the earth dwellers who curse God (16:9, 11, 21) and the beast who blasphemes God's name (13:6). The praise and worship is usually from those in heaven who say/speak out (4:8), or sing (5:9), or cry out in a loud voice (7:10) or shout (19:1). Heaven is a place for new songs because the Lamb has redeemed men for God, and in 14:3 (cf. 5:9) the redeemed themselves sing a new song that only they can sing, where both angels and elders sing a new song together.

Angels themselves not only praise God for who he is, but also praise in response to events on earth (e.g., 19:4–5), and praise in relation to events not yet happened (e.g., 7:1–12). As Noll says, it is the great response to, "thy will be done"; the only possible answer to what God does on earth.[4]

Angels praise with humanity. The cycle of praise in Rev 4 and 5 has a building quality to it, where one group inspires the next. The living creatures begin by constantly proclaiming "*Holy, holy, holy is the Lord God Almighty, who was, and is, and is to come.*" (4:8). This is responded to by the elders laying down their crowns, and crying out: "You are worthy, our Lord and God, to receive glory and honour and power, for you created all things, and by your will they were created and have their being" (4:11).

Yet if God is worthy, then creation needs to respond to this. There is a scroll to be opened, but nobody can—not even an angel. Only the Lamb can, and he ascends the throne and takes the scroll. Now the Lamb is worshipped by the four living creatures, the elders, the angels (with harps), and every creature in heaven and the earth *singing* to the Lamb as Redeemer (5:9–10). This is followed by the myriads of angels crying:

---

4. Noll, *Angels of Light*, 191.

"Worthy is the Lamb, who was slain, to receive power and wealth and wisdom and strength and honour and glory and praise!" (5:12).

Finally, in praise of God (the Father) and Christ, all creatures—including the angels—call out, which the living creatures conclude by saying, "Amen!" (5:13), before the Elders fall down in worship (5:14). Following this incredible round of responsorial praise by humans and angels—heaven and earth—the next praise event centres on the great multitude *crying out* in praise of the Lamb for their salvation (7:10), followed by the angels, the elders, and the four living creatures also worshipping God (7:12).

Yet, this amazing event is then followed by half an hour of silence, when John saw the angels offering prayers and incense to God (8:1–5), before the seven angels sounded their seven trumpets. But this silence is as important as the praise beforehand. Sometimes, in worship, we need a period of silence to present one's prayers to God. After the seventh trumpet is sounded, the time of eschatological fulfilment has come. It is declared loudly by the voices of the redeemed who come to heaven to join with the angels (11:15). Then the elders worship God, but there is no mention of the angels joining in, except maybe as some of the heavenly voices. "We give thanks to you, Lord God Almighty, the One who is and who was, because you have taken your great power and have begun to reign. The nations were angry; and your wrath has come. The time has come for judging the dead, and for rewarding your servants the prophets and your saints and those who reverence your name, both small and great—and for destroying those who destroy the earth" (11:17–18).

The lack of angelic voices here maybe reflected in the fact that after this praise, which is speaking of earthly events, God's temple was opened and the sacred chest of the covenant was seen—a covenant with humans not angels (11:19). And this earthly focus continues through the next chapters, although it does include the heavenly battle between Michael and Satan, with Satan being thrown down to earth. We then reach the 144,000 *singing* a new song before the throne, the four living creatures, and the elders. However, no one could learn the song except the 144,000 who had been redeemed from the earth (14:3)—not even the angels, but they nevertheless accompany them on harps. Some songs are unique to some groups, but this doesn't mean involvement by others in praise ceases.

Those victorious over the beast, his image, and his followers then *sing* the song of Moses the servant of God and the song of the Lamb (15:3–4). The defeat of the beast was an occasion for praise and declaring truth, and the temple was filled with smoke and the glory of God! (15:8) Next, the bowls of wrath are poured out, and Babylon falls—God's great judgment comes to pass in absolute clarity. What is the reaction of heaven to this horrific sight? It is the hallelujah chorus that is *shouted* by a great multitude in heaven. This includes the saints, the elders, and the four living creatures. "*Hallelujah! Salvation and glory and power belong to our God, for true and just are his judgments.* He has condemned the great prostitute who corrupted the earth by her adulteries. He has avenged on her the blood of his servants." And again they shouted: "*Hallelujah!* The smoke from her goes up for ever and ever." The twenty-four elders and the four living creatures fell down and worshipped God, who was seated on the throne. And they cried: "*Amen, Hallelujah!*" (Rev 19:1–4).

This worship is notable because it sees judgment, and from that also sees the good work of God to right what is wrong in the world. Judgement comes with avenging condemnation, and this is a cue for worship. Yes, the eternally burning city brings forth worship. Strangely this is the last mention of worship in heaven by the four living creatures and the elders and even of the saints, and the last round of worship comes from a great multitude. God's people are now cleansed and pure, ready for the wedding feast of the Lamb, and praise God loudly with great joy (19:5–8).

It is perhaps odd that worship of this kind is not mentioned in the last chapters. Previously, the dominant word for worship had the root *proskuneō* / προσκυνεω, which has the sense of prostration, falling down, and coming before, in worship (e.g., 7:11; 11:16; cf. 4:10; 5:14). However, Rev 22:3 says "and his servants will *serve* him." The root of this word for "serve" is *latreuo* / λατρευο and it means to minister to God, render religious service, to worship, to perform sacred services. In Heb 9:9 and 10:2 it is translated as worshipper. The word seems to have a more active sense to it than *proskuneō*. The explanation for the change in word might be explained by the fact that we will live with God, with the angels, in the heavenly city (Heb 12:22–23). All worship in heaven now changes to something else. It moves from passive prostration to lively service. The response to God's action on earth and in history is now left behind, and something new is created. His servants, who are angels and humans, serve him with a living and active *latreuo*.

So, what can we learn from all of this? It all seems so wonderful, but of little relevance to us here on earth. How is this related to us, here and now? What can angels teach us through this? I think there are five main points to draw from it:

1. Their worship is not without relationship to the truth—it states truth! And this truth is about the nature and character of God. We see this also in Isa 6 where the angels call to each other the Triashagion of *Holy, Holy, Holy!*

2. The worship of the angels is not shown as un-rooted in the events in the world around them. They praise in response to events, both good and bad, and not about vague or idealised notions about God's wonderfulness. Praise comes when God is acting at the sharpest ends of human history and sin: both judgment and salvation draws forth praise, and both deliverance and a burning city inspire worship.

3. Their worship is also not unrelated to others praising. It is not an individualistic, selfish, lonely event, but always communal. Angels inspire us to praise God, and they praise with us. They watch and enjoy others praising, and they accompany praise of others. God's reconciled community of angels and humans, are as one in praise and worship. Angels enjoy, and are humble in letting us worship with them. Just as there is joy over one sinner repenting, so they have joy about reconciled sinners now praising.

4. Sometimes, we need silence to be a part of our wider worship and honor of God. Even in heaven there was silence while prayers were presented to him.

5. Our worship will become a living, heavenly lifestyle with the angels, in the New Jerusalem. It is not just songs, but a life lived with God.

The worship given by angels is related and relational, neither dislocated nor abstracted from reality, but rather resting directly within God's true and wider reality. Our worship too should show the same awareness of the eternal transcendent action of God, rooted in and declaring truth about God, responding to events around us, and related to the Christian community around us. Worship is not just something which heightens our emotions (which it can), but is a lifestyle, as Paul's tells us in Rom 12:1. The disciplined life of love and forgiveness is an act of worship. The godly life lives with reconciliation at the forefront of the mind. We have seen how angels help us live that godly life pleasing to God. How also can angels be a part of the reconciling process here on earth?

FORGIVENESS AND RECONCILIATION WITH GOD

While the process of living the Christian life could be called an on-going act of reconciliation through confession and repentance, the ultimate and foundational act of reconciliation one can have in this life is to be reconciled to God through Christ. We have already seen how the post-Pentecost role of angels was to drive on evangelism and the ever wider spread of the gospel. Angels point us to Christ, leading the church to preach Christ, and so move people toward that truly reconciled and forgiven life. Yet once people have this one, single, destiny-changing act of reconciliation, they also have to have many smaller acts of reconciliation throughout life. Life is one long act of on-going reconciliation, of protecting and renewing our relationship with God and neighbor, not forgetting that angels also walk with us.

Consider the angel that sustained a scared and burnt-out Elijah on his journey to Horeb to meet with God, where he was re-commissioned and reinvigorated (1 Kgs 19). Elijah has his ministry renewed, and finds an apprentice, successor, and companion—Elisha. The angel was a vital part of the process which returned Elijah to God.

However, central to any reconciliation is honesty and openness, and, crucially, confession. Confession is the basis for all true, deep reconciliation. And angels can play a role in this in our lives. Isa 6:1–7 spells this out with amazing clarity and detail, and the dynamics of this passage are very important. Isaiah sees God on his throne surrounded by the seraphim praising him. The smoke is the tangible visible presence of God, and in the midst of this scene, Isaiah realises the incredible sinfulness of both himself and his nation, and he cries out in desperation and confession to God. Note, that in response to Isaiah's heart cry, the angel is sent by God with a coal, and with the coal touched his mouth and said: "Behold, this has touched your lips; your guilt is taken away, and your sin atoned for."

This is worth emphasising. For while Isaiah called out to God, and the coal came from God's altar—and so God is the ultimate source of the forgiveness and cleansing—the heavenly being was the vehicle by which this was applied to Isaiah. God did not do it directly, but used his seraphim to do it for him. A classic example of heavenly beings as God's secondary means. The angel came and ministered forgiveness to Isaiah by both touch and declaration, and this event was the catalyst for Isaiah's long and illustrious prophetic ministry. This formula of touch and declaration is also mirrored in both the calling and gifting of Jeremiah where God touched his mouth (Jer 1:9), and the opening of Daniel's mouth when silenced by the awesome vision of the fiery figure (Dan 10:16).

A similar event is spoken of in Zech 3:4, where Joshua the High Priest, standing clothed in dirty garments, was accused by Satan. The Angel of the LORD was there, and spoke: "And the angel said to those who were standing before him, 'Remove the filthy garments from him.' And to him he said, 'Behold, I have taken your iniquity away from you, and I will clothe you with pure vestments.'"

The angel, like the heavenly creatures in Isa 6, was used to remove Joshua's sin and make him, in God's eyes, clean again. These actions mirror the role of the human priest in confession. Properly understood, confession is where one can unburden oneself in a safe environment, and then have somebody stand with you and pronounce the truth of 1 John 1:9: "If we confess our sins, he is faithful and just to forgive us our sins and to cleanse us from all unrighteousness."

Angels do not provide forgiveness, and are not the source of forgiveness, but they are involved in God's work of cleansing people. Maybe this is a reason why one sees carvings of angels on the mercy seat (Exod 25:17–22; Num 7:89). Angels can lead us to confession and repentance (for example, through their holy lives bringing self-reflection), and the pronouncement of God's truth of forgiveness over us. Just as when we stand with somebody in confession and declare God's truth to them, so do the angels, who provide that same comfort and assurance to us.

RECONCILIATION WITH NEIGHBOR

Alongside reconciliation with God comes reconciliation with neighbor, the reconciliation of one person with other people. How do angels support us in this? We have looked at the areas of angels and the promotion of the godly life, and angels and forgiveness—and these are two aspects of reconciliation, but are there more?

Forgiveness and reconciliation with God are directly linked to forgiveness and reconciliation with your neighbor. Jesus made clear that one cannot happen without the other: "So if you are offering your gift at the altar and there remember that your brother has something against you, leave your gift there before the altar and go. First be reconciled to your brother, and then come and offer your gift" (Matt 5:23–24).

Note the direction of the reconciliation: if someone holds anything against you, then you are responsible to sort it out. You do not wait for them to come to you.

One example of angels assisting in this process is with Hagar and Sarai (Sarah) in Gen 16. The breakdown of relationship is abundantly clear from the text. Both parties had a part to play in it, with Abram (Abraham) compliant and weak on the sidelines. Accusations flying, recriminations are let loose, and finally Hagar runs away. However, an angel finds Hagar, and tells her to return ("submit") to Sarah (16:6–9). The word translated "submit" in many Bibles is a poor translation. Its literal meaning is more to be humble and live in acceptance of one's lower place (Heb: *hit'anni*). It is to have a modest opinion of oneself, to be unassuming, and to live one's life in the light of that. It is not a command to be subordinated so that you are a slave or servant.[5] The angel is not telling Hagar to submit like a slave. Previously Hagar's attitude was positive to her mistress (16:4–5), but once pregnant she became proud and started to despise Sarah. The angel is therefore telling her to return to Sarah with a renewed attitude, and a right and humble approach to her mistress, not just simply to serve and obey. The angel told Hagar to amend her thinking to a more godly pattern, and in this way begin the journey of reconciliation between her and Sarah. It is a command for inner change, not outward conformity. It was a piece of pastoral guidance, discipline and correction, not a demand for obedience.

The depth of this reconciliation is not clearly spelt out, but it is was only when Isaac was born some thirteen or so years later (Gen 21) that Sarah seems to have reignited the flames of fallout and driven Hagar and Ishmael away again. The conflict was not of Hagar's making. The word of the angel seems to have profoundly reshaped her attitudes, and this was a long-lasting impact which allowed blessing upon her and Ishmael's lives.

---

5. The root of the word used by the LXX (*tapeinoō* / ταπεινόω) arises in the New Testament in Phil 2:8, where Christ humbled himself, and in Mary's song in Luke 1:48 that she is a humble servant girl. It is *not* the word, for example, found in passages such as Gal 2:5; Rom 8:20; or 1 Pet 2:13, 18 (root: *hupotassō* / ὑποτάσσω).

A RECONCILED COMMUNITY

We are called to be reconciled to God and neighbor, but also we are called to be within a reconciled society and community. God's love, forgiveness and healing is not for the holy-huddle or the elect elite, but for the whole world. So one may ask the broader question, *What is a healthy society and relationship? What do these look like?* Here one could begin to reference and develop the thinking behind the idea of a united society of angels and humans, as indicated in Heb 12:22–24, and believed in by Jewish groups like the Essenes. This is a passage rich with meaning and depth, and a powerful context. It is preceded by the rather bleak picture in 12:18–21, where the readers are told they have not come to Sinai, a place not to be touched, a place of fire, darkness, gloom and whirlwind, where no-one could bear the trumpet sound, nor the voice of God. Instead: "You have come to Mount Zion and to the city of the living God, the heavenly Jerusalem, and to innumerable angels in festal gathering, and to the assembly of the firstborn who are enrolled in heaven, and to God, the judge of all, and to the spirits of the righteous made perfect, and to Jesus, the mediator of a new covenant, and to the sprinkled blood that speaks a better word than the blood of Abel" (Heb 12:22–24). There is a direct contrast made, and Lane makes clear this shift in the text. As Christians we do not look at the physical Mount Sinai because: "Christians order their lives in accordance with a different revelation."[6]

By virtue of accepting the gospel, the readers have come to the spiritual realm described—to Mount Zion. Mount Zion was the royal residence of David (2 Sam 5:6–10), and the religious centre of the kingdom where the Ark was (2 Sam 6:2ff.). It was the earthly dwelling place of God (1 Kgs 14:21; Ps 78:68), and where Israel met to worship. And just as the earthly Zion was the meeting point for the tribes of the old Israel, so the heavenly Jerusalem is the meeting point for the new Israel.[7] It echoes the New Jerusalem of Rev 21:2, but whereas that passage focuses on the "not yet" aspects of the city, the passage in Hebrews stresses the "now" aspects of this life. In the spiritual realm believers have access to it, the city which is to come (Heb 13:14). Bruce writes: "The privileges of its citizenship are already enjoyed by faith. The people of God are still a pilgrim people . . . but by virtue of His sure promise they have already

---

6. Lane, *Hebrews 9–13*, 464.

7. Bruce, *Hebrews*, 356.

arrived in spirit."[8] It is an image of the promise in Eph 2:6, where we will be seated with Christ in the heavenly realms, with immediate impact and meaning in our lives. As Christians, we already enjoy in the present the eschatological city of the future.[9]

Where have they arrived? To myriads of angels in festal array, in joyous assembly. Myriads echo both Deut 33:2 and Dan 7:10, with their pictures of the whole host of heaven before God. The word translated as festal or joyful has many echoes. It has religious overtones (Ezek 46:11; Hos 2:11; 9:5; Amos 5:21), as well as hinting toward to the marriage supper of the Lamb (Rev 19:6–7). This is not the dark picture of 12:18–21. Furthermore it is not just a meeting of angels: "By coming to Mount Zion and the New Jerusalem, they of course mingle with the inhabitants of this divine city. These are of two kinds: angelic and human."[10]

They have also arrived at a wider community. This community, described as *ekklesia*, which has the sense of "church," includes the *first born* and the *spirits of the righteous*. The firstborn might be the angels, but this is not likely since they have already been mentioned. It is more likely to be those whose names are written (enrolled) in heaven (Luke 10:20). The spirits of the righteous are probably the pre-Christian believers mentioned in 11:39–40. These two terms then point to the entire communion of saints—the men and women of faith of both covenants.[11] It is crucial to note that this is not just talking about presence within, but actual membership of, the heavenly community. It cannot be taken away, but is yours for eternity, because you are enrolled, and there is a union of angels and God's people in a worshipping fellowship. Lane paints a wonderful picture: The weight of the passage "falls on the density of the angelic population, as innumerable multitudes gathered in plenary assembly for an exultant celebration of worship . . . The Heavenly Jerusalem is a place of blessing, where the redeemed can join with angels, archangels and all the company of heaven in celebratory worship of God."[12]

The passage as a whole says that God is no longer unapproachable, nor dread-inspiring as on Sinai. He dwells among a worshipping society,[13]

8. Ibid., 357

9. Hagnar, *Hebrews*, 225.

10. Brown, *Hebrews*, 652.

11. Ibid., 360.

12. Lane, *Hebrews*, 467.

13. Guthrie, *Hebrews*, 261.

and the outcome of this oneness of society under God is radical. It is a society of holiness and love, which functions in a perfectly—and literally, heavenly—way. As Guthrie sums up: "The author's picture of the gathered assembly at Mount Zion communicates exultation, warmth, openness, acceptance, and relationship."[14]

It worth reflecting on these last five words—exultation, warmth, openness, acceptance, and relationship. This is what any godly community should look like. This is the fruit of reconciliation active within a community and society, and in this context the idea of the single reconciled heavenly community gains extra weight.

There are two very different groups in the sights of this passage—human and angelic. One is holy and spiritual, one sinful and fleshly, yet both with a single destiny of the heavenly Jerusalem. A common idea over the centuries has been that the fall of the angels was rooted in the rejection of the incarnation because it involved such a close relationship of God with lesser beings—humans—and their subsequent exaltation to heaven alongside the angels.[15] Satan rebelled at such diminution of the angelic nature, and having to share not only heaven with humans, but also have their nature raised up to be like and equal with his own. His pride and abhorrence at human nature caused his fall, but was not reflected by two thirds of the other angels who saw the joy and wonder that we can only get a glimpse of in this passage. While this is speculative, it does provide an image of how divergent and different angels and humans are. Yet if holy angels can minister to sinful humans as diligently and obediently as they do, so we humans should do the same for others whatever their condition. The angels' humility and service to us should prick our consciences to serve and love those whom the world around would deem as too low to be worth helping.

The heavenly community is one of praise and worship, it is God-focused, and it is praying. It is a diverse and mixed community of various peoples, cultures, and groups all together in one place, doing one thing, demonstrating both unity and love amid their differences. It is a place of no pain and tears, and the community lives in such a way that this never happens. What an example to emulate.

14. Guthrie, *Hebrews (NIV)*, 420.

15. E.g., Hooker, *The Laws of Ecclesiastical Polity* V: App 1:29; Irenaeus, *Demonstration of the Apostles' Teaching.* 16; Gregory of Nyssa: *Great Catechism*, 6:5.

In heaven, angels rejoice at our repentance. The reconciled community takes pleasure in seeing the lost brought into this community (Luke 15:10). It is a joy which they seek and a pleasure they work towards. It is their delight to see God restore and bless those alienated and far from him. On earth we too should take pleasure in being a part of that reconciling work and community. The impact of the reconciled community, not only stretches between heaven and earth, but from within the church to those beyond, with the ultimate goal to draw them into this heavenly society and life with God.

And the core of this heavenly society—angels and humans, Old and New Testament believers, Jews and Gentiles, men and women—is the one mediator, Jesus Christ (12:24). It is his sacrifice and his blood which enables this one society to exist. Col 1:12–22 speaks of this clearly. All things were created by Jesus, the angels in the heaven and the humans on earth. While angels are not explicitly mentioned in this passage, Colossians as a whole deals with righting a skewed view of spiritual powers, and asserting a correct understanding of them in relation to (i.e. *under*) Christ (cf. 2:8, 18, 20), therefore the "all" used in Col 1, to make sense, must include the totality of the spirit and angelic realms. Thus, angels "good and bad" are subject to Christ.[16] Col 1:20 teaches that "all of existence is united in Christ"[17] through his death, by which the "whole universe (is) restored to its God ordained destiny"[18], which surely must include the good angels as well as bad. Simply, "the reconciliation wrought by Christ extends to the entire cosmic order."[19]

All things—angels and humans—exist and are held together by Jesus. Most importantly, all things in heaven and on earth (including the Church of which he is head) were reconciled to the Father by his blood, and his sacrificial death on the cross was for angels and humans to be one and at peace with each other and with God, holy and blameless. The angels have this now, we will have it when we are in glory, and then together, holy and blameless through Christ, we will live in the reality of Heb 12:22–23. We both worship for the same reason, that we are both ultimately reconciled to God through Christ. We are not so different from our angelic brethren, and this is why they are our brethren. If you want

16. Bruce, *Colossians*, 63–64.

17. Melick, *Philippians, Colossians*, 229.

18. Harris, *Colossians*, 46.

19. Patzia, *Ephesians, Colossians*, 33.

to know what a truly Christian society looks like, you could do worse than meditate on Col 1:12–22 and Heb 12:22–24 and the huge richness of the images they contain.

Here is the completion of the pastoral process. When we are reconciled to Christ and readied for our new life with him in heaven, fully restored, fully healed, and fully united, the angels have played their part, and done their job for him. They too will rest in glory, as we will rest in glory, and we will live together serving God in the new heavens and new earth. And there, I suspect, we will share stories of the wonders of God, the glory of Christ, and the work of the Spirit. We will rejoice in everything he has done for us, and thank him for taking us on a journey through life together. There we will know as we are known, and we humans will thank God for our angelic brethren.

$$\approx \quad 9$$

In the Shadow of Their Wings

As this book neared completion, I began to wonder how I would end it. What would I say in the final and concluding chapter? While I pondered this, life carried on as usual, and one day I found myself at the Warneford Hospital in Oxford, attending a seminar on mental health chaplaincy. While at college training for the ministry, I was doing a placement in one of the local secure wards, learning how one works with people with mental health difficulties. It was a placement which taught me many new skills, exposed weakness in some I already had, and encouraged growth in others. The people I worked with were often very damaged and disturbed, having faced many awful situations and found they couldn't cope. Human wreckage sat before my eyes in a real and painful way. And yet, in the midst of this suffering I was always taken aback by the hope shown, and the search for God. One may expect injured souls to despise and reject God, but more often than not the opposite is the case. These people would patiently queue up, waiting for a chat with the chaplain. The world had no answers—they had found this out in the hardest way possible. But maybe the transcendent, the spiritual, maybe even God himself, had the answers they were looking for.

As I sat in the chapel listening to the teaching (which was very good), I suddenly felt a light bulb go on in my head—maybe an angel had flicked a switch inside my brain! While we were being taught what good people skills for mental health chaplaincy looked like, a slide had come up on the projector with the following words:[1]

---

1. With thanks to Rev Steve Bushell, who not only led the seminar and created this list, but also supervised my placement in the Warneford Hospital.

SPIRITUAL SKILLS

- Relational—empathetic listening.
- Imaginal—able to work with the symbolic.
- Still—to be fully present in a calm manner.
- Attentive—able to attend to four dimensions (physical, mental, emotional, spiritual)
- Open—to the transpersonal/divine/cosmos.
- Alive—to feelings.
- Respectful—of the humanity of others.
- Gratitude—all life-experiences are opportunities for spiritual growth.
- Wonder—open to a sense of wonder and awe.

Next to the projected image of the slide on the wall were two beautiful icons—one of Rubelev's three angels depicting the Trinity, and one, I think, of the Archangel Michael. My eyes saw the image and icons, my mind made a connection, and my spirit leapt. Here was a way to end the book.

The list described the skills and character traits one needed to work with people who have severe mental health issues. Mental health, in its most extreme form, could be considered as being at the extreme end of pastoral care, the place where the rubber truly hits the road, and one's gifts and abilities are tested to the maximum.

Using a totally different framework, if angels have the skills on this list, then angels can do any pastoral care we may wish to throw at them. Here is the cutting edge. Can angels work at this edge?

- *Relational*—one of the most striking things which I discovered while writing this book was how good angels' people skills are. Often they did not rely simply on their awesome presence to get things done, but listened, chatted, answered questions, calmed doubts and fears, encouraged, and blessed. Angels are incredibly relational beings.

- *Imaginal*—I read through the visions given by angels to Zechariah, and knew instantly that angels could not only speak in symbols, but guide us through those symbols, so we can gain deeper meaning from them. One can say the same of the angel helping John through Revelation. More than plain words, symbols speak deeply, and angels can help us understand those symbols and their mysteries.

- *Still*—I have often pictured the two angels sitting on the stone rolled away from Jesus' tomb, calmly waiting for somebody to come and ask what was going on. I can similarly picture the angel sitting under the tree waiting for Gideon to notice him and start a conversation. No rush or hurry, knowing that the right time will come. Gabriel gave both Mary and Daniel time and space to adjust to their monumental angelic meetings, gently guiding them into understanding and blessing.

- *Attentive*—Angels are always aware that their presence can produce incredible reactions of fear, wonder, and confusion, which can impact a person in numerous ways. Their presence can make people weak, so they pick them up and strengthen them. Their presence can cause confusion, so they speak into situations with truth and clarity. Their presence can cause panic, so they say "*Do not fear!*" And their presence can lift you into a whole new understanding of the breadth of God's creation, the riches of his glory, and the wonders of his purposes.

- *Open*—In the introduction I mentioned a quote by Francis Schaeffer who said that in every conversation, mention angels, since by this people's eyes are pulled away from moral and ethical religion of law into the realms of a transcendent and supernatural faith. Angels, by their very existence, open our eyes to the riches of the unseen cosmos. They open our eyes, minds, and souls to the simple fact that there is more than what we can see.

- *Alive*—Angels have feelings like us. They rejoice when one sinner repents and comes to know Jesus. They feel the dismay when nobody can open the scroll, and also the joy welling up to praise when the Lamb steps forth and claims the scroll. Angels are not cold inscrutable beings, but experience emotion like us.

- *Respectful*—Angels do not need to trample over people in order to do God's will. They clearly have the power to do so, but would rather go at our pace, answering our questions in a way to put us at ease. Again, how Gabriel spoke with both Mary and Daniel demonstrates this beautifully.

- *Gratitude*—All life experiences are opportunities for spiritual growth. The worship of God by the angels throughout Revelation was in reaction to both the judgement and sin on the world, and the glory and intervention of God in response. We too can know that a spirit open and aware of what God is doing in the world can do nothing but elicit praise and thanks to him.

- *Wonder*—In the same way that angels allow us to be open to the spiritual and transcendent, they also open us to a sense of wonder and awe. We are not alone, and there is more, so much more, than our physical eyes can see.

C. S. Lewis made the oft repeated comment, that there are two equal and opposite dangers when considering demons—either to ignore or reject them completely, even deny their existence, or to so over focus on them that they dominate one's mind, thought, and theology. Lewis called for a balanced view of demons which fell into neither trap. In the same way, this book calls for a re-evaluation of angelology, which has generally fallen into similarly polarised camps. These polarised camps worry, at one extreme, about angels being demons in disguise and misleading people, or about folk-religion and bad teaching around them arising and obscuring Christ. At the other extreme, some may say that the presence of angels in our preaching, spirituality, liturgy and Scriptures can demonstrate an unnecessary irrationality which drives people away from God in a rational society. Neither extreme is required, and this book, I hope, starts to chart a new course which can rightly place angels back on the spiritual map, under God and under Christ, not as something to run from or avoid, but to embrace as one part of God's glorious creation which he has given for our blessing.

I know that for much of this book, I have been reading biblical passages in a way which is quite alien to traditional methods. For example, it would not be the most natural focus of the dialogue between Gideon and the angel to consider the fact that the angel came, sat, and waited for him under the tree, and what this would look like in a pastoral context.

Neither is it particular common in hermeneutics to look at the role of the touch the angel gave a frightened and fleeing Elijah when he was in the wilderness. Nor is it usual to look at how angels drove the initial mission of the church, both encouraging disciples in the face of persecution, and launching them and the gospel beyond Jerusalem, to Judea, Samaria, and the ends of the earth. Yet I believe that it is a natural way to read the texts—seeing angels primarily as beings who *do*, and only to secondarily wonder about what they *are* and how they exist. I equally believe that to read the biblical witness and only arrive at speculative bewilderment which buries serious theology and eliminates angels from our spiritual vision does no justice to how God presents angels to us in Scripture.

Angels, in all they do, point us toward God, and post-Pentecost, specifically to the Lord Jesus Christ. They can do no other, because they are the ministering spirits sent to serve those who will inherit salvation, a salvation which is found by only one name in heaven and on earth—Jesus. This is the Name before whom every knee will bow, and every tongue will confess. Angels confess this, we confess this. They are our brothers and fellow-servants, and if God wishes them to serve us while we sojourn here on planet earth, then I for one can only be grateful and thankful to God.

Adler, M. J. *Angels and Us*. London: MacMillan, 1988.

Alexandra (Mother). *Holy Angels*. Minneaoplis: Light & Life, 1987.

Allen, L. C. *Ezekiel 1–19*. Word Bible Commentary. Waco, TX: Word, 1994.

Aquinas, Thomas. *Summa Theologiae*. London: Eyre & Spottiswoode, 1963–1972.

Arndt, W. F., and F. W. Gingrich. *A Greek English Lexicon of the New Testament and Other Early Christian Literature*. London: Cambridge University Press, 1957.

Barth, K. *Church Dogmatics. Vol III: Doctrine of Creation*. Edited by G. W. Bromiley and T. F. Torrence. Edinburgh: T. & T. Clark, 1960.

Barton, J., and J. Muddiman, editor. *The Oxford Bible Commentary* Oxford: Oxford University Press, 2007

Berkof, L. *Systematic Theology*. Grand Rapids: Eerdmans, 1953.

Block, D. I. *The Book of Ezekiel*. New International Commentary on the Old Testament. Grand Rapids: Eerdmans, 1997.

Bradshaw, P. *Companion to Common Worship II*. London: SPCK, 2006.

Bramhall, J. *Works of John Bramhall*. Vol IV. Library of Anglo Catholic Theology. Oxford: John Henry Parker, 1845.

Brenton, L. C. L. *The Septuagint with Apocrypha: Greek And English*. Grand Rapids: Zondervan, 1980.

Breward, I. *The Works of William Perkins*. Berkshire: Sutton-Courtnay, 1970.

Brown, F. Driver S., et al. *The Brown-Driver-Briggs Hebrew-English Lexicon*. Peabody, MA: Hendrickson, 1995.

Brown J. *An Exposition of the Epistle to the Hebrews*. London: Banner of Truth, 1961.

Brownlee, W. H. *Ezekiel 1–19*. Word Biblical Commentaries 28. Waco, TX: Word, 1986.

Bruce, F. F., *The Book Of Acts*. New International Commentary on the New Testament. Grand Rapids: Eerdmans, 1988.

———. *The Epistle To The Colossians, To Philemon, and To The Ephesians*. New International Commentary on the New Testament. Grand Rapids: Eerdmans, 1984.

———. *Hebrews*. New International Commentary on the New Testament. Grand Rapids: Eerdmans, 1991.

Bruckner, J. K. *Exodus*. New International Bible Commentary. Peabody: Hendrickson, 2008.

Bulgakov, S. *The Orthodox Church*. Crestwood, NY. St Vladamir's Seminary Press, 1988.

Bulgakov, S. *Jacob's Ladder*. Grand Rapids: Eerdmans, 2010.

Bultmann, R. *Theology of the New Testament*. Translated by Kendrick Grobel. 2 vols. London: SCM, 1952.

———. "New Testament and Mythology." In *Kerygma and Myth, vol. I*, edited by H. W. Bartsch, 1–44. London: SPCK, 1964.

Butler, J. *The Analogy of Religion Natural & Revealed*. London: Dent., 1906.

Calvin, J. *Institutes of the Christian Religion*. Translated by H. Beveridge. Grand Rapids: Eerdmanns, 1994.

Cambridge History of Judaism Vol 2 (The Hellenistic Period) Cambridge: Cambridge University Press, 1999.

Cambridge History of Judaism Vol 3 (The Roman Era) Cambridge: Cambridge University Press, 1999.

Campbell, A. *A Dictionary of Pastoral Care.* London: SPCK, 1993.

Carson, D. A. *Matthew 13-28.* Expositor's Bible Commentary. Grand Rapids: Zondervan, 1995.

Catholic Catechism. London: Chapman, 1994.

Christou, S. *Informed Worship.* Cambridge: Phoenix, 2009.

Clebsch, W., and C. Jaekle. *Pastoral Care in Historical Perspective.* New York: Aaronson, 1964.

Clines, D. J. A. *Job.* In *New Bible Commentary,* edited by D. A. Carson et al, 459–84. Leicester, UK: InterVarsity, 2005.

Colish, M. L. *Peter Lombard.* 2 vols. Leiden: Brill, 1994.

Common Worship. London: Church House, 2000.

Common Worship (Festivals). London: Church House, 2008.

Common Worship (Pastoral Services). London: Church House, 2004.

Danielou, J. *The Angels and Their Mission.* Translated by David Heimann. 1952. Reprint, Westminster: Christian Classics, 1982.

Davidson, M. J. *Angels at Qumran.* Sheffield, UK: JSOT Press, 1992

Davies, H. *Worship and Theology in England,* Vol. 5. London: Oxford University Press, 1965.

Descartes, R. *Meditations.* Edited by J. Cottingham. Cambridge: Cambridge University Press, 1996.

Durham, J. I. *Exodus.* Word Biblical Commentaries 3. Waco, TX: Word, 1987.

Eichrodt, W. *The Theology of the Old Testament.* Translated by J. A. Baker. Vol. 2. London: SCM, 1967.

———. *Ezekiel.* Translated by Cosslett Quin. London: SCM, 1970.

Ellingworth, P. *The Epistle To The Hebrews: A Commentary On The Greek Text.* New International Greek Testament Commentary. Carlisle, UK: Paternoster, 1993.

Elwell, W., ed. *Baker's Evangelical Dictionary of Theology.* Grand Rapids: Baker, 1996.

Ferguson, S. and D. F. Wright. *New Dictionary of Theology.* Leicester, UK: InterVarsity, 1991.

Flusser, D., and A. Yadin, *Judaism of the Second Temple Period the Jewish Sages and Their Literature.* Grand Rapids: Eerdmans, 2009.

Glenn, P. J. *A Tour of the Summa.* Rockford, IL: Tan, 1978.

Goll, J. W., and M. A. Goll. *Angelic Encounters.* Lake Mary, FL: Charisma House, 2007.

Graham, B. *Angels.* Dallas: Word, 1986.

Green, J. *The Gospel Of Luke.* NICOT. Grand Rapids: Eerdmans, 1997.

Grimm, C. L. W., and J. H. Thayer. *A Greek English Lexicon of the New Testament.* Edinburgh: T. & T. Clark, 1890.

Grudem, W. *Systematic Theology.* Leicester, UK: InterVarsity, 1994.

Guthrie, D. *Hebrews.* Tyndale New Testament Commentary. Leicester, UK: InterVarsity, 1986.

Guthrie, G. H. *Hebrews.* NIV Application Commentary. Grand Rapids: Zondervan, 1998.

Hagnar, D. A. *Hebrews.* New International Bible Commentary. Peabody, MA: Hendrickson, 1990.

Hannah, D. D. *Michael & Christ.* Wissenschaftliche Untersuchungen zum Nueuen Testament 2/109. Tübingen: Mohr/Siebeck, 1999.

Harbury, W. *Jewish Messianism & The Cult of Christ.* London: SCM, 1998.

Harris, M. J. *Exegetical Guide to the Greek New Testament: Colossians and Philemon* Grand Rapids: Eerdmans, 20101.

Hastings, A. *The Oxford Companion to Christian Thought.* Oxford: Oxford University Press, 2000.

Hobbes, Thomas. *Leviathan.* Edited by E. Curley. Indianapolis: Hackett, 1994.

Holladay, W. L. *A Concise Hebrew and Aramaic Lexicon of the Old Testament.* Grand Rapids: Eerdmans, 1996.

Hooker, Richard. *Of the Laws of Ecclesiastical Polity.* 2 vols. Edited by C. Morris. London: Dent, 1969.

Isaacs, R. H. *Ascending Jacob's Ladder (Jewish Views of Angels, Demons, and Evil Spirits)* New Jersey: Aaronson, 1997

Keck, D. *Angels and Angelology in the Middle Ages.* New York: Oxford University Press, 1998.

Keener, C. S. *Revelation.* NIV Application Commentary. Grand Rapids: Zondervan, 2000.

Kittel, G., editor. *Theological Dictionary of the New Testament.* Vol. 4. Grand Rapids: Eerdmans, 1967.

Küng, H. *The Church.* Translated by Ray and Rosaleen Ockenden. New York: Image, 1976.

———. *On Being a Christian.* Translated by Edward Quinn. London: Collins, 1978.

———. *Eternal Life.* Translated by Edward Quinn. London: Collins, 1984.

———. *Does God Exist?* Translated by Edward Quinn. London: Collins, 1980.

Lane, A., editor. *The Unseen World.* Carlisle, UK: Paternoster, 1996.

Lane, W. L. *Hebrews 9–13.* Word Bible Commentary 47B. Waco, TX: Word, 1991.

Langton, E. *Supernatural.* London: Rider, 1934.

Lartey, E. Y. *In Living Color: An Intercultural Approach to Pastoral Care and Counselling.* London: Kingsley, 2003.

Liddel, H. G., and R. Scott. *A Greek English Lexicon.* Oxford: Clarendon, 1976.

Locke, John. *An Essay on Human Understanding.* Philadelphia: Kay & Troutman, 1849.

Lombard, Peter. *Works of Peter Lombard.* Patrologia Latina 192. Paris: Migne, 1880.

Lossky, V. *The Mystical Theology of the Eastern Church.* London: Clarke, 1957.

Louth, A. *Denys the Aeropagite.* London: Chapman, 1989.

Luz, U. *Matthew 8–20.* Hermeneia. Translated by James E. Crouch. Minneapolis: Fortress, 2001.

Macy, J. *Angels in the Anglican Tradition (1547–1662).* PhD diss., King's College, London, 2003.

———. *How Does the Liturgy of the Church of England Present a Pastoral Theology of the Angels: From the Book of Common Prayer to Common Worship?* MTh thesis, Wycliffe Hall, Oxford, 2009.

McQuarrie, J. *Principles of Christian Theology.* London: SCM, 1977.

Melick, R. R. *Philippians, Colossians, Philemon.* New American Commentary 32. Nashville: Broadman, 1991

Morris, L. *Matthew.* Leicester, UK: InterVarsity, 1992.

———. *Revelation.* Leicester, UK: InterVarsity, 1983.

———. *Luke.* Leicester, UK: InterVarsity, 1997.

———. *Revelation.* Tyndale New Testament Commentary. London: Tyndale, 1971.

Morton, M. *Personal Confession Reconsidered (Making Forgiveness Real).* Nottingham, UK: Grove, 1994.

Mounce, W. D., and R. H. Mounce. *A Greek English Interlinear New Testament (NIV/ NASB).* Grand Rapids: Zondervan, 2008.

New Patterns For Worship. London: Church House, 2002.

Noll, S. F. *Angels of Light Powers of Darkness.* Downers Grove, IL: InterVarsity, 1998.

Nolland, J. *Luke 18:35—24:53.* Word Bible Commentary 35C. Nashville: Nelson, 1993.

Noth, M. *Exodus.* London: SCM, 1966.

On Holy Angels. Canada: Synaxis, 1990.

Owen, H. P. *Revelation and Existence.* University Of Wales Press, 1957.

Pannenburg, W. *Systematic Theology.* Vol. 2. Translated by Geoffrey W. Bromiley. Grand Rapids: Eerdmans,1994.

Pagels, E. *The Origin of Satan.* New York: Random House, 1995.

Parente, P. *The Angels.* Rockford, IL: Tan, 1994.

Patzia, A. G. *Ephesians, Colossians, Philemon* New International Biblical Commentary. Carlisle, UK: Paternoster, 2004

Pelikan, J., and H. Lehmann. *Luther's Works.* Philadelphia: Fortress, 1958–1986.

Price, H. *Angels: True Stories of How They Touch Our Lives.* London: Pan, 1994.

Rahner, K. *Encyclopaedia of Theology.* London: Continuum, 1975.

Richardson, A., and J. Bowden. *A New Dictionary of Christian Theology.* London: SCM, 1983.

Roberts, A., and J. Donaldson, editors. *Ante-Nicene Christian Library.* Peabody, MA: Hendrickson, 1995

Rorem, P. *Pseudo-Dionysius.* Oxford: Oxford University Press, 1993.

Schaff, P., and H. Wace, editors. *Nicene and Post Nicene Fathers.* Peabody: Hendrickson, 1995.

Schleiermacher, F. *The Christian Faith.* Edinburgh: T. & T. Clark, 1928.

Schriener, S. *The Theatre of His Glory.* Lynnwood, WA: Labyrinth, 1991.

Strauss, F. D. *The Life of Jesus, vol. I.* Translated by M. Evans. New York: Blanchard, 1860.

Taylor, J. B. *Ezekiel.* Tyndale Old Testament Commentary. London: Tyndale, 1971.

Theilicke, H. *The Evangelical Faith.* Grand Rapids: Eerdmans, 1982.

Tillich, P. *Systematic Theology.* Chicago: University of Chicago Press, 1951.

Vermes, G. *Jesus the Jew.* London: Fontana, 1977.

Virtue, D. *Messages from Your Angels.* London: Hay House, 2002.

Wakefield, G. S. *A Dictionary of Christian Spirituality.* London: SCM, 1983.

Wall, R. W. *Revelation.* New International Bible Commentary. Peabody, MA: Hendrickson, 1991.

Ware, K. *The Orthodox Way.* Oxford: Mowbray, 1981.

———. *The Orthodox Church.* London: Penguin, 1987.

Warren, F. E. *The Sarum Missal in English.* 2 vols. London: Mowbray, 1913.

Wesley, John. *Sermons.* Vol. 2. Edited by T. Jackson, London: Kershaw, 1825.

Williams, P. S. *The Case for Angels.* Carlisle, UK: Paternoster, 2002

Wink, W. *Engaging the Powers.* Minneapolis: Fortress, 1992.

———. *The Powers that Be.* New York: Doubleday, 1998.

———. *Unmasking the Powers.* Minneapolis: Fortress, 1986.

———. *Naming the Powers.* Minneapolis: Fortress, 1984.

Woodward, J., and S. Pattison. *Blackwell Reader in Pastoral & Practical Theology.* Oxford: Blackwell, 2007.

Wright, C. J. H. *The Message of Ezekiel.* Bible Speaks Today. Leicester, UK: InterVarsity, 2001.

Wright, N. T. *Surprised By Hope.* London: SPCK, 2007.

———. *Resurrection and the Son of God.* London: SPCK, 2003.

Young, E. J. *The Book of Isaiah, Vol. 3, Chapters 40–66.* Grand Rapids: Eerdmans, 1973.

Genesis

1:1	9
1:3	9
1:4	9
1:31	9
3:24	11, 13, 111
6:1ff.	11, 120
16:4–9	137
16:7	13
16:7–12	55, 71, 80, 117
16:9	112
16:10–13	14
18:10	75
18:16	11
19:1–22	75, 119–20
19:10–11	120
21	137
21:1	75
21:17–18	55, 71, 80, 124
21:20–21	117–18
22:11–18	71, 75
24:7	13, 118
24:40	118
25:24–34	107
27	107
27:36	107
28	26, 64
28:10–22	107–8
28:16–17	64
31:11	13
31:11–13	14, 75, 108
32:1	108
32:24–30	108
32:30	75
48:15–16	13, 108–9

Exodus

3:2–4	71, 75
14:19	71
19:6	102
23:20–23	71, 73, 83
25:18–20	130, 136
25:22	130, 136
26:1	130
26:31	130
31:10	21
32:23	72
32:34	71
33:2–3	71, 72
33:12ff.	72
33:20	74
34:6–7	72
37:7–9	130
39:1	21

Leviticus

20:3	101
22:24	115
25	109

Numbers

4:12	21
4:26	21
7:5	21
7:89	130, 136
22:22ff.	11
22:31–35	112
24:2	113
23:4	113
23:5	113
23:16	113
24:1	113

Lightning Source UK Ltd.
Milton Keynes UK
06 April 2011
170449UK00002B/74/P